STUDENT WORKBOOK FOR

REFLECT & RELATE
An Introduction to Interpersonal Communication

STUDENT WORKBOOK FOR

REFLECT & RELATE
An Introduction to Interpersonal
Communication

Third Edition

by Steven McCornack

Prepared by Jennifer Samonte Valencia
Design Institute of San Diego

Bedford/St. Martin's
Boston ◆ New York

Preface

There is much to learn and practice in an introductory interpersonal communication course. This Student Workbook for *Reflect & Relate*, Third Edition, is designed to help you learn the content and practice the skills covered in your textbook. Therefore, the workbook focuses on three areas: *recalling* information from your textbook, *practicing* interpersonal communication skills, and *relating* what you have learned to your life. Every chapter of the workbook contains the following elements:

- **Study Outline.** To help you learn the material in each chapter, the outline guides you through the chapter, highlighting the major points and asking you to fill in missing key terms and concepts.

- **Vocabulary Help.** I often hear that one of the main challenges in studying interpersonal communication is the amount of vocabulary one has to learn. To help you master key terms, each chapter contains two exercises:

  - **Word Search.** In this fun exercise, clues point to vocabulary terms hidden in the word search.

  - **Defining Key Terms.** Here you will be asked to explain vocabulary terms in your own words.

- **Case Study.** This activity presents you with a brief scenario about interpersonal communication and then asks five guided questions to help you critically assess the situation.

- **Self-Test.** To help you prepare for exams and check your comprehension of the chapter material, this quiz asks you 20 true or false questions. You may check your score using the Answer Key at the end of the manual, which also provides the textbook page number the question came from.

- **Journal Entry.** Critical self-reflection is an important part of applying interpersonal communication concepts to your own life; these questions prompt you to reflect on your own experiences with the material.

—Jennifer Samonte Valencia

Contents

STUDENT WORKBOOK FOR

REFLECT & RELATE
An Introduction to Interpersonal Communication

STUDY OUTLINE

Fill in the blanks to complete the outline.

I. What Is Communication?

   A. The National Communication Association defines **communication** as the process through

     which people _____

     _____

     _____.

   B. There are five features that characterize communication:

     1. First, communication is a _____.

     2. Second, communicators use _____ to convey meaning.

       a. When people exchange a series of messages, whether face-to-face or online, the

         result is called an _____.

     3. Third, communication occurs in an endless variety of situations, known as

       _____.

     4. Fourth, people communicate using various _____.

     5. And finally, communicators use a broad range of tools, known as _____.

C. The Communication Process

    1. The **linear communication model** contains five components: _____,

    _____, _____, _____, and

    _____.

    2. The **interactive communication model** builds on the first five components of the linear

    model but includes _____ and _____.

    3. The most refined model is the **transactional communication model**. The major

    difference in this model is that _____

    _____.

II. What Is Interpersonal Communication?

    A. **Interpersonal communication** is defined as _____

    _____.

    B. There are four components of the definition:

    1. Communication is *dynamic*, meaning that _____.

    2. Interpersonal communication is also _____.

    3. Third, communication is **dyadic**, meaning _____.

    4. Interpersonal communication changes the participants' _____,

    _____, _____, and _____.

      a. In perceiving relationships as **I-Thou**, we _____

      _____.

      b. In perceiving relationships as **I-It**, we _____

      _____.

C. **Impersonal communication** has a(n) _____ on our thoughts, emotions, behavior, and relationships.

D. There are five general principles of interpersonal communication:

    1. Interpersonal communication conveys both _____ and

    _____.

        a. Interpersonal communication can include a specific form of _____, which is defined as communication about communication.

    2. Interpersonal communication can be either _____ or

    _____.

    3. Interpersonal communication is _____.

    4. Interpersonal communication is _____.

E. Three different types of goals motivate interpersonal communication: **self-presentation, instrumental**, and **relationship goals**.

    1. These goals address _____ needs, _____ needs, and _____ needs.

    2. Self-presentation goals are _____

    _____.

    3. Instrumental goals are _____

    _____.

    4. Relationship goals are _____

    _____.

F. Communication scholars usually take one of two approaches in conducting *research*.

1. Qualitative approaches involve _____

_____.

2. Quantitative approaches involve _____

_____.

III. What Is Interpersonal Communication Competence?

A. **Interpersonal communication competence** is communication that meets three essential

criteria: the communication is _____, _____, and

_____.

B. Repeatable goal-directed behaviors and behavioral patterns that you routinely practice in

your interpersonal encounters and relationships are called _____.

C. **Appropriateness** is the degree to which _____

_____.

1. We judge how appropriate our communication is through _____.

2. *High self-monitors* are people who _____

_____

_____.

3. *Low self-monitors* don't _____

_____.

D. **Effectiveness** is the ability to use communication to _____

_____.

E. **Ethics** is defined as _____

_____.

IV. Improving Your Competence Online

    A. Understanding and adapting to online norms is the first step in developing interpersonal competence online.

        1. Scholar Malcolm Parks offers five suggestions for improving online competence.

           a. Match the gravity of your message to your _____.

           b. Don't assume that online communication is always _____.

           c. Presume that your posts are _____.

           d. Remember that your posts are _____.

           e. Practice the art of creating _____.

V. Issues in Interpersonal Communication

    A. Culture is the set of _____

      _____.

    B. Gender consists of _____.

        a.   Each of us also possesses a _____.

    C. Our ability to communicate easily and frequently, even when separated by geographic distance, is further enhanced through _____.

    D. The fact that relationships can bring us joy obscures the fact that _____ _____.

WORD SEARCH

Each of the following clues describes one of the components of the models of communication. Write the term in the space provided, and then find it hidden in the word search.

1. Waving your hand, saying "Hello," or writing a note that says "Hello." _____.

2. Wearing cologne and burning scented candles while entertaining company at your home.

   _____.

3. Responding to criticism with a frown, or saying "I disagree." _____.

4. A crowded room, 12 p.m., on a rainy day. _____.

5. Kids screaming in the background, the sun's glare, someone's strong perfume.

   _____.

6. The president when delivering a speech or your mother when she tells you to clean your room.

   _____.

7. A student being told that he/she did a good job or a worker being reprimanded for being late.

   _____.

8. The belief that running is fun, the value that hard work brings fortune, the bad attitude that all

   men are alike. _____.

```
E K U M N Z X R U W C I Y O Y B E X B P M H
O C N F T U E S I O N O W J E O A F F C E V
O W N E L V H J Y U M G N B G E G D C N S S
P O B E E U L T I R G Q I T L S H Q A Q S S
D R Q I I D V U T M Y L E H E M A A F L A E
Q M C Y D R S S U Y H D H K J X U D X D G C
U E P J S Z E X C T K G L W V X T U Z H E I
R E B R K O W P H J U K E K O O L R V V P K
J D C A C Q O R X A N O A J S J J Y D S V K
O N O Z A P E L A E Y Z T H V P K W P D I A
X D S Q B R D H S Q F S C Z X C N P X W I E
J I O U D Q C T Y L E O P Z K W A X G R P G
L X Y I E C H A N N E L S W L W D Y F H G U
G K J L E M D X D T H Z W D Q O T B U A X L
M Q Y S F R N E G F F W T G L M E N E J W W
H B Z E O P R F Z Y L E Z O D E X P L N S P
N B Z F O K S E T D U D F Z A P I X B U Q U
K R G I Z U S W P M K U F N O N S F I R X M
I W Y S X P P O I P X V B D O S F I G A K A
W H P R K N P N L B M A U K F R M V X V P W
W Z A A I G X Z Z W M Y E M L B B A B L H L
A E M E H N M E C R Q H N M C K A Q T J L U
```

DEFINING KEY TERMS

Write a sentence that defines each of the following key terms.

1. Communication _____

   _____

2. Ethics _____

   _____

3. Online communication _____

   _____

4. Interactive communication model _____

   _____

5. Interpersonal communication _____

   _____

6. Intrapersonal communication _____

   _____

7. Dyadic _____

   _____

8. Meta-communication _____

   _____

9. Gender _____

   _____

10. Interpersonal communication competence _____

    _____

I-Thou _____

_____

2. I-It _____

_____

CASE STUDY

Read and analyze the following case study, and then answer the questions regarding the principles of communication.

Grayson, age 5, and Leila, age 2, are playing together with building blocks. Grayson is building a large fortress-like structure, while Leila is building a simple stack of blocks. Grayson has run out of blocks and says to Leila, "I need some of your blocks for my tower," while removing blocks from her stack. In response, Leila knocks over Grayson's fortress with a pout. Grayson then growls at Leila, who runs off crying.

1. According to the principles of communication, what content information is being conveyed in the scenario above?

2. How does each communicator display relationship information? What does it indicate about how they view their bond?

3. What intentional and/or unintentional message(s) could Grayson have been trying to send to Leila by growling at her?

4. What are some of the outcomes that this communication scenario might have on Grayson and Leila's relationship? If scenarios similar to this occur repeatedly, what implications might it have for their future relationship?

5. What is an example of how a similar situation might occur in an adult relationship?

SELF-TEST

For each of the following sentences, circle T if the statement is true or F if the statement is false.

T F 1. Communication occurs through channels and within contexts.

T F 2. Interpersonal communication is exclusively defined as communication between two people.

T F 3. Communication has an indirect effect on our relationship outcomes.

T F 4. The linear model of communication accounts for the feedback we receive during communication.

T F 5. The transactional model of communication depicts a "good" way to communicate.

T F 6. The linear model of communication shows information flowing in only one direction.

T F 7. The interactive model of communication suggests that transmission is influenced only by feedback and fields of experience.

T F 8. In the transactional model of communication, there aren't senders or receivers, but rather, all participants are viewed as co-communicators.

T F 9. A defining factor of interpersonal communication is that it primarily involves a dyad (two people).

T   F   10. I-Thou communication means that the speaker views the other communicator as more sophisticated.

T   F   11. When using I-It communication, we increase the likelihood that we'll communicate in disrespectful, manipulative, or exploitative ways.

T   F   12. Strengthening interpersonal communication competence includes consistently communicating in ethical ways.

T   F   13. Content is conveyed primarily through verbal interaction.

T   F   14. Interpersonal communication can help us achieve each of the levels of Maslow's hierarchy of needs.

T   F   15. Meta-communication means pretending to communicate.

T   F   16. Relationship outcomes can be determined by communication choices.

T   F   17. Online communication is always more efficient than face-to-face conversations.

T   F   18. Gender influences how people communicate interpersonally.

T   F   19. Content information includes nonverbal displays that add meaning to your words.

T   F   20. Overemphasizing appropriateness can hurt both the communicator and those around him or her.

JOURNAL ENTRY

Have you ever experienced a misunderstanding that resulted from using online communication inappropriately or ineffectively? When have you benefited from online communication? Give specific examples.

_____

_____

_____

_____

_____

_____

_____

_____

_____

_____

_____

_____

_____

_____

_____

_____

_____

_____

_____

_____

STUDY OUTLINE

Fill in the blanks to complete the outline.

I. The Components of Self

A. The **self** is _____

_____.

B. **Self-awareness** is the ability to _____

_____.

1. **Social comparison** involves observing and assigning meaning to others' behavior and

then _____.

2. Critical _____ can greatly enhance your interpersonal

communication.

C. **Self-concept** is your overall perception of _____.

1. Self-concept is based on the _____, _____, and

_____ you have about yourself.

2. The impact that labeling has on our self-concepts was termed the

_____ by Charles Horton Cooley.

3. **Self-fulfilling prophecies** are predictions about future interactions that lead us to behave in ways that ensure that interaction _____ _____.

D. **Self-esteem** is the _____.

   1. **Self-discrepancy theory** suggests that your self-esteem is determined by how you compare to two mental standards: your _____ and your _____.

   2. You can improve your self-esteem using the following five steps:

      a. First, assess your _____.

      b. Next, analyze your ideal self by answering the question: _____ _____?

      c. Third, analyze your ought self by answering the question: _____ _____?

      d. Fourth, revisit and redefine your _____.

      e. Finally, _____.

II. The Sources of Self

A. **Gender** is the composite of _____, _____, and _____ that characterize us as male or female.

   1. Scholars distinguish between gender, which is largely _____, and biological sex, which _____.

   2. Immediately after birth, we begin a lifelong process of _____.

B. Our communication and interaction with family shape our beliefs about interpersonal relationships.

1. Our _____ play a crucial role in the formation of our self-concept, providing us with a ready-made set of beliefs, attitudes, and values.

2. One dimension of attachment is _____, the degree to which a person fears rejection by relationship partners.

3. The degree to which someone desires close interpersonal ties is called

_____.

4. Four attachment styles are _____,

_____, _____, and

_____.

C. **Culture** is another powerful source of self.

1. Culture is defined as _____

_____.

2. In **individualistic cultures**, people are encouraged to focus on _____

_____.

3. In **collectivist cultures**, people are taught _____

_____.

III. Presenting Your Self

A. Others' impressions of you are based mostly on your _____ and behavior.

B. Your _____ is the public self you present whenever you communicate with others.

C. We create different faces for different moments and relationships in our lives.

1. A **mask** is a public self designed to _____

_____.

2. We form a strong emotional attachment to our face because it represents _____

_____.

3. Loss of face provokes feelings of shame, humiliation, and sadness, also known as

_____.

D. During online interactions, the amount of information communicated is radically

_____ and more easily _____.

1. People often present themselves online in ways that amplify

_____, such as _____, _____,

and _____.

2. The downside of online communication is that unless you have met someone in person,

you will have difficulty _____

_____.

3. _____ suggests that when assessing someone's online

self-descriptions we consider the _____ of the

information presented.

a. Information that can't be verified offline has _____.

b. Information that can be readily verified offline has _____.

E. Three practices can improve online self-presentation.

1. First, keep in mind that online communication is dominated by

_____.

2. Second, always remember the important role that _____ plays

in shaping others' impressions of you.

a. One simple rule: what others say about you online is _____

than what you say about yourself.

3. Finally, subject your online self-presentation to the _____

test.

IV. The Relational Self

A. **Social penetration theory** envisions the self as an _____

structure consisting of sets of_____, with the "safest" characteristics

on the outside and distinctive personality traits at the core.

1. The _____ layers of your self are demographic characteristics.

2. The _____ layers include your attitudes and opinions about music,

politics, food, and entertainment.

3. Core characteristics are in the _____ layers.

4. _____ is the number of different aspects of self each partner reveals at

each layer.

5. _____ involves how deeply into each other's self the partners have

penetrated.

6. Depth and breadth of social penetration are intertwined with _____: the

feeling of _____ that exists between us

and our partners.

B. The Johari Window has four quadrants: _____,

_____, _____, and

_____.

C. The act of disclosing your self to others plays a critical role in interpersonal

communication.

1. **Self-disclosure** involves revealing _____ about ourselves to

others.

2. According to the _____, the closeness we feel toward

others in our relationships is created through _____ and _____

_____.

3. Intimacy only exists when both people are _____

_____.

4. Culture and gender impact self-disclosure.

a. In any culture, people vary widely in the degree to which they _____.

b. People across _____ differ in their self-disclosure.

c. People disclose more _____, _____, and

_____ when interacting online than face-to-face.

(i) Be wary of the _____ qualities of online interaction.

d. Self-disclosure appears to promote _____ and relieve

_____.

e. Gender-based stereotypes about self-disclosure are not supported by evidence. For

instance, in close same-same sex relationships, _____ disclose broadly

and deeply. However, both genders are more willing to disclose to _____

recipients.

D. The text offers six recommendations for effectively disclosing your self:

1. Follow the advice of Apollo: _____.

2. Know your _____.

3. Don't force others to _____.

4. Don't presume _____.

5. Be sensitive to _____.

6. Go _____.

WORD SEARCH

Each of the following clues describes terminology about the components of self. Write the term in the space provided, and then find it hidden in the word search.

1. A comprehensive view of the answer to the question "Who am I?"_____.

2. "He works out every day and is so healthy; I never work out." "She dresses so grungy every day; I, on the other hand, like to wear designer clothes that are clean and ironed." These are examples of _____.

3. Gregory thinks he is really good at jiu jitsu. He enters the dojo with confidence and is aggressive and focused. His positive attitude contributes to an outstanding victory over a much less self-assured opponent. Gregory goes home thinking, "I knew I would win!" This is an example of _____.

4. William believes that others think he's a great athlete, so he formulates an image of himself in his mind as fit, agile, and exceptionally strong, even though he might be scrawny, slow, and uncoordinated. This is an example of _____.

5. The ability to step outside yourself and view yourself as a unique person distinct from your environment is _____.

6. In her mind, Corazon thinks she should be responsible and frugal. Others also expect her to be organized and punctual. This theory suggests that she might feel low self-esteem if she views herself as irresponsible, frivolous, disorganized, and always late.

_____.

```
S L F G S T W Q U I B N Z S G Y Y R L T W Y
H O U K Z A S Q Q D M H E B F I P U A G C I
K O C B N K M A G M T L B C H N K M M E N F
U K M I T W C B R E F W P T G D X B H C R G
G I Z U A S V U Z A M N P C Y C O P Q I C D
I N H I K L Z G W B S N D X R J O P R D Z B
P G R S I V C A E V J B V W F R P F I M J P
G G O P S R O P K Q I N S P T B E N L Z W
I L K U G E X W M E E D K G G C F Q K O H N
U A Y R N D A F D P D M N Y X K C Y P F C A
K S F E F Q A G T I A I F B H B L L G X Q N
D S S E N I P H V R L R C O A E N T F P K Z
H S M Y A E W U T L R N I N T H C X K F W A
Z E A L W C Y W I A N D A S T C N C F U H M
B L I P X C W F J T P E C N O C F L E S O I
W F N X H J L F J L L R M C U N X D H W Y H
C Z H P E U R L T O Q T M S N X S Y G B W N
L C H Y F H P A G X E C A B V E S M F J M C
Q J C F A Y K B X G D F O X D I C B B C R X
T H L G W A I A L D V H O A Q U H J D X N I
S E L F D I S C R E P A N C Y T H E O R Y M
S I C F L C D J I N R Q G T I V L I P J A B
```

DEFINING KEY TERMS

Write a sentence that defines each of the following key terms.

1. Self _____

_____

2. Self-esteem _____

_____

3. Gender _____

_____

4. Secure attachment _____

_____

5. Preoccupied attachment _____

_____

6. Culture _____

_____

7. Individualistic culture _____

_____

8. Face _____

_____

9. Mask _____

_____

10. Social penetration theory _____

_____

11. Warranting value _____

_____

12. Self-disclosure _____

_____

CASE STUDY

Read and analyze the following case study. Answer the questions regarding self-disclosure.

Troi wants to introduce his friend, Gerry, to his coworker, Arlene. Troi gives Gerry Arlene's e-mail address and encourages him to contact her. Over the next few weeks, Gerry and Arlene exchange dozens of e-mails, sometimes four or five in one day. They write about superficial topics like the weather and the news, but more often, they write about intimate thoughts, feelings, and emotions. An e-mail relationship blossoms, and finally Gerry and Arlene plan to meet for the first time and spend a weekend together at a cabin in Lake Tahoe. They feel comfortable doing this because they've gotten to know each other quite well via e-mail. Troi thinks the relationship seems to be moving quite rapidly, since they have never met in person, and voices his concerns—to no avail.

1. In this case, how is self-disclosure affected by the online nature of Gerry and Arlene's relationship?

2. What type(s) of online mask(s) play a role in this scenario? What types of masks may Gerry and Arlene be utilizing?

3. How would Gerry and Arlene self-disclose differently if they met first in a face-to-face manner?

4. What do you think are the benefits of self-disclosure via online interactions?

5. What do you think are the disadvantages of self-disclosure via online interactions?

SELF-TEST

For each of the following sentences, circle T if the statement is true or F if the statement is false.

T F 1. The United States is a highly collectivist culture.

T F 2. Your face is the self that you reveal only to your closest friends.

T F 3. In the Johari Window model, our public area of self is initially much smaller than our hidden area.

T F 4. When hanging out with your school friends, you pretend that you are interested in politics because you don't want to be excluded from their conversations and because you've heard them talk negatively about apolitical peers. Your efforts to appear interested in politics are known as a mask.

T F 5. The three components of self are self-awareness, self-concept, and critical reflection.

T F 6. Gender socialization refers to the process of learning from others about what it means to be male or female.

T F 7. Social penetration theory describes layers of information that you reveal about yourself ranging from basic facts to private feelings.

T F 8. When dealing with online communication, it is always appropriate to disclose information.

T F 9. Women tend to disclose more than men.

T F 10. A good starting point for improving your self is to "know thyself."

T F 11. Tendencies to disclose are influenced by culture.

T F 12. You should always assume that Asian people will not disclose as much as Europeans.

T F 13. Self-disclosure appears to promote stress and anxiety.

T F 14. A police officer who pretends to be a 12-year-old girl online in order to catch sexual predators is wearing a mask online.

T F 15. Everyone in Cody's family realizes he's an alcoholic, but Cody is in denial. This information is in the blind area of his Johari Window.

T F 16. It is always ethical to disclose as long as you're being honest.

T F 17. Once formed, self-esteem is impossible to improve.

T F 18. Online, people tend to present themselves in the best manner possible.

T F 19. Scott has a Facebook account that has several pictures of him partying wildly with friends. This could potentially affect his job search efforts.

T F 20. While working, Gary dresses and speaks in a professional way. This is considered a mask.

JOURNAL ENTRY

Make an assessment of your online self-presentation. Google your name, and consider any screen names and profiles (Facebook, Web pages, blogs, etc.). If you were a complete stranger looking at your profile, what assumptions would you make about the person behind the profile? If you were a potential employer, would you hire yourself? Why or why not?

_____

_____

_____

_____

_____

_____

_____

_____

_____

_____

_____

_____

_____

_____

_____

_____

_____

_____

_____

_____

_____

_____

Name: _____

Class: _____

Date: _____

STUDY OUTLINE

Fill in the blanks to complete the outline.

I. Perception as a Process

    A. The process of **perception** has three parts:

        1. The first step in perception is_____. In this step, we focus our

           attention on certain _____

           _____.

           a. The degree to which particular people or aspects of their communication attract our

              attention is known as _____.

        2. In **organization**, the second step, you take the information you've selected and_____

           _____

           _____.

           a. During organization, you engage in _____ to structure the

              information into a chronological sequence.

        3. The final step, _____, means that we _____

           _____.

a. We make sense of others' communication in part by comparing _____

_____ with _____

_____.

b. **Schemata** are _____

_____. These are what we draw on when

interpreting interpersonal communication.

c. As a part of interpretation, we create explanations for others' comments or behaviors.

These explanations are known as _____.

(i) _____ presume that a person's communication comes

from internal causes.

(ii) _____ presume that a person's communication stems from

factors unrelated to personal qualities.

d. The **fundamental attribution error** is our tendency to attribute others' behaviors

to_____

_____.

e. The _____ is the tendency of people to

make external attributions regarding their own behaviors.

f. We typically take credit for success by making an internal attribution known as the

_____.

g. _____ explains why crediting ourselves for our life successes

makes us happier about who we are.

h. Normally, communication stems from both _____ and

_____ causes.

B. Sometimes people communicate in ways we find perplexing.

1. When we feel that we can't explain or predict someone's communication, we

   experience _____, which is especially common during

   _____.

2. According to **Uncertainty Reduction Theory**, _____

   _____.

3. Uncertainty can be reduced in several ways.

   a. Passive strategies for reducing uncertainty include _____

      _____.

   b. Active strategies include _____

      _____.

   c. The most direct and effective way of easing uncertainty is using

      _____.

II. Influences on Perception

   A. The culture in which you were raised influences your perception of others.

      1. People raised in different cultures have different knowledge in their

         _____, so they interpret one another's communication in very

         different ways.

      2. Your schemata are filled with _____, _____,

         _____, and _____ you learned in your own

         culture.

      3. Culture affects whether you perceive others as _____ or _____.

         a. **Ingroupers** are people whom you consider _____

            _____.

    b. **Outgroupers** are people _____.

4. We are more likely to give valued resources such as money, time, and effort to—

   and to form positive interpersonal impressions of—those who are perceived as

   _____.

B. The relationship between gender and perception is more complicated than our stereotypes

   would have us believe.

1. The difference in cerebral cortex structure allows women to more accurately

   _____.

2. Canary, Emmers-Sommer, and Faulkner concluded that men and women respond in a

   similar manner _____ percent of the time when it comes to interpersonal

   communication.

3. One thing we know for certain about gender and perception is that _____

   _____.

C. **Personality** is another factor in how we perceive people.

1. Personality is an individual's characteristic way of _____,

   _____, and _____,

   _____.

2. The "Big Five" personality traits are _____, _____,

   _____, _____, and

   _____.

3. Our perception of others is strongly guided by _____

   _____.

4. We evaluate people positively or negatively in accordance with

   _____.

5. _____ are personal beliefs about different

types of personalities and the ways in which traits cluster together.

6. Presuming that someone is high or low in one trait because he or she is high or low in

others can lead you to _____

_____.

III. Forming Impressions of Others

A. _____ are mental pictures of who people are and how we feel about

them.

B. A **Gestalt** is a(n) _____

_____.

1. Gestalts are useful because they form _____ and require

_____.

2. Examples of _____ include people believing pleasant events are

more likely to happen than unpleasant ones.

3. When Gestalts are formed, they are more likely to be positive than negative, an effect

known as the _____.

4. The **negativity effect** occurs when _____

_____.

5. The main idea behind the **halo** and **horn effects** is that _____

_____.

C. **Algebraic impressions** differ from Gestalts in that _____

_____.

D. One last way we form impressions is by using _____, which is a term that describes overly simplistic interpersonal impressions.

    1. One negative outcome of stereotyping is that it causes us to _____

    _____.

    2. Stereotyping can also create _____

    _____.

IV. Improving Your Perceptions of Others

    A. One of the most valuable tools for communicating more effectively with others is

    _____, which we experience when we _____

    _____.

    1. *Perspective-taking* is the ability to _____

    _____.

    2. *Empathic concern* encompasses the _____ of considering

    _____.

    3. Experiencing empathy isn't sufficient to improve interpersonal communication and

    relationships. You must also _____.

    B. Another way to improve perception is to embrace **world-mindedness**, defined as _____

    _____

    _____.

    C. The opposite of world-mindedness is _____, defined as _____

    _____.

    D. **Perception-checking** involves five steps:

    1. Check your _____.

2. Check your _____.

3. Check your _____.

4. Check _____.

5. Check your _____.

WORD SEARCH

Each of the following clues is a key term from Chapter 3. Write the term in the space provided, and then find it hidden in the word search.

1. Josephine's friend Priscilla just lost her grandmother to breast cancer. Even though Josephine herself has never lost a family member to cancer, she can see why Priscilla is so sad. This is an example of showing _____.

2. Upon seeing Jacinda for the first time, Stefani sees she is well-groomed, poised, and articulate. Stefani forms an all-encompassing positive first impression called a _____.

3. Because Stefani had a positive first impression of Jacinda, when Jacinda burps, Stefani thinks it's charming. This is an example of the _____ effect.

4. Rachel has been trying to quit smoking. As she scans the newspaper, a tiny advertisement for a smoking clinic jumps out at her. Her attention to the ad because of its importance to her reflects the ads's _____.

5. Khanh says that he made Desiree fall in love with him after he charmingly tripped over her dog at the park. Desiree says that she made Khanh fall in love with her after she helped him nurse his sprained ankle. Khanh's and Desiree's different ways of sequencing and organizing information are an example of _____.

6. When Marcos describes his car as a low-rider, Angelica visualizes it in her mind before she sees it. The mental pattern she uses to make the information familiar is called a(n) _____.

7. Jaylynn joins a stay-at-home mothers' online forum and finds that she shares many similarities with the other members, such as an interest in scrapbooking, their family situations, and their membership in the group. She views the other mothers as _____.

8. Adolfo is quiet, shy, kind, and easygoing. These traits that guide the typical way he thinks, feels, and acts are parts of his _____.

```
Y T V Y X P T W G Q S T Z C X W A B C M Z X
J T I U X R W X E D R C T N U E R O N T U U
G J I E R G M X O H E V U L L D U X W P Q W
R G P L M P Y P K A P N R G L H D K E I X X
R G H O A P J J V Q U J X O O S C C R E Y E
K P G Q V N A Z N A O I G S R O N A B K G O
S Z J C T K O T W O R W E W G E H F V K R K
F O G N I W R S H K G J S Z I A A S X K T R
R K F H J D Z J R Y N Y T L L Y H C G F M W
C L R R O O C M B E I J A O Y I Y X C V L L
K K V K O F S W X W P S L T Z E X P X H X W
U X N R H T F H V L Q W T U M T U G P C X R
E C G C Z U W H J W B O I W R K E M S R D L
S C H E M A T A M W P J I T B Z J B B Q Z T
M X S G Z O M A Z X T K G B O R V R A J S C
R Z M H V P P L G C F Q X L D V I I I B U X
B U B X Y U H Y X X D D J K C Z W J H G Q K
F N X Q Y R X S M P N Q M O C C B F F Q Z K
N O I T A U T C N U P H T Y W V J L K I R L
E G U P D G I R D U N E U T C D W Q G M W T
S D Y P I Y W T I Z G H O X X G C D U H I S
M D H G P Y T G S N V D E C J R C R R Y A C
```

DEFINING KEY TERMS

Write a sentence that defines each of the following key terms.

1. Fundamental attribution error _____

_____

2. Actor-observer effect _____

   _____

3. Uncertainty Reduction Theory _____

   _____

4. Implicit personality theories _____

   _____

5. Interpersonal impressions _____

   _____

6. Positivity bias _____

   _____

7. Negativity effect _____

   _____

8. Self-serving bias _____

   _____

9. Horn effect _____

   _____

10. Algebraic impressions _____

   _____

11. Perception-checking _____

   _____

12. Ethnocentrism _____

   _____

Read and analyze the following case study, and then answer the questions regarding how we form impressions of others.

Sam is at a picnic with his friends. There are many people Sam doesn't know at the picnic, so he strikes up a conversation with the most extroverted girl, Trang. Upon meeting Trang, Sam immediately likes her; she seems funny and smart, not to mention attractive. Trang, on the other hand, is slow to form an impression about Sam and spends much of the day observing his behavior and asking friends questions about him. She finds out he works hard as a plumber and has a large family, and she observes that he is pretty funny. So far, he seems like a good guy. As the day wears on, however, Sam starts drinking more and gets in an altercation when he loses at a game of horseshoes. At the end of the day, Sam asks Trang for her number. Trang feels conflicted because he seemed like a nice guy at first, but he then got into a fight with someone.

1. What type of Gestalt has Sam formed about Trang? What factors did he base this Gestalt upon?

2. What role did the positivity bias play in the impressions that Sam has formed of Trang?

3. What role did the negativity effect have on Trang's impression of Sam?

4. As Sam formed a Gestalt about Trang, explain how Trang developed an algebraic impression of him.

5. Do you think Trang believes that Sam's drinking and the fight he got into are related? Why or why not?

SELF-TEST

For each of the following sentences, circle T if the statement is true or F if the statement is false.

T   F   1. Algebraic impressions are formed quickly.

T   F   2. An example of the fundamental attribution error would be to assume that a coworker has often been late recently because he's lazy, not because he's been up late with his newborn baby.

T   F   3. Being empathetic means feeling sorry for someone.

T   F   4. People you consider fundamentally similar to yourself are called ingroupers.

T   F   5. When you see a cloud formation in the sky, and it resembles your old dog, you are in the organization stage of perception.

T   F   6. We tend to place extra importance on the first information we receive about a person.

T   F   7. You are more likely to notice a billboard for a debt consolidation company if you are having money problems. This is an example of high salience.

T   F   8. Shariff blames Charlotte for crashing their car, but Charlotte insists that she got in an accident because Shariff distracted her. This is an example of differences in punctuation.

T   F   9. The process of perception-checking can help you avoid errors in judgment.

T   F   10. Cara thinks that it is uncivilized when her friend Manny eats with his hands, a commonly accepted practice in his culture. Cara is being ethnocentric.

T   F   11. When we can't predict or anticipate people's communication, we become more uncertain and tend to form negative impressions of them.

T   F   12. Our own personality influences our perception of the traits we possess, but not how we perceive the traits of others.

T F 13. Forming a Gestalt is the most accurate way to form an impression of someone.

T F 14. Race is a way we classify people based on descent, and race is almost entirely determined by looking at physical features.

T F 15. Everyone, regardless of race, perceives racial distinctions in the same way.

T F 16. Due to innate differences, men and women are vastly different in their interpersonal communication styles.

T F 17. The implicit personality theory suggests that we presume that because someone is high in one aspect (friendliness, for example), he or she is high in other areas (extraversion, openness) also.

T F 18. We stereotype because it streamlines the perception process.

T F 19. The first step in perception-checking is checking your impressions.

T F 20. Due to the halo effect, we are surprised whenever someone exhibits positive qualities.

Write about a situation in which you felt that you were classified as an outgrouper. What inaccurate stereotypes do you think the ingroupers made about you? Now, think about a time when you classified someone else as an outgrouper. Did you view them, their actions, or their communication positively or negatively? On what did you base this perception?

_____

_____

_____

_____

_____

_____

_____

_____

_____

_____

_____

_____

_____

_____

_____

_____

_____

_____

_____

_____

CHAPTER 4

Experiencing and Expressing Emotions

STUDY OUTLINE

Fill in the blanks to complete the outline.

I. The Nature of Emotion

  A. Defining Emotion

    1. Emotion is an intense reaction to an event that involves

      _____,

      _____,

      _____,

      _____, and

      _____

      _____.

      a. Emotion is reactive, which means it is triggered by

        _____.

      b. Emotion involves _____, in the form of increased heart

      rate, blood pressure, and adrenaline release.

c. To experience emotion, you must become_____

_____.

d. How we each experience and express our emotions is constrained

by _____, _____,

_____, and_____ norms, which

govern _____.

e. When emotion occurs, the choices you make regarding emotion management are

reflected outward in_____in the form of

_____.

2. Emotion is communicative in that we talk about our _____

with _____, a form of communication known as

emotion-sharing.

3. **Emotional contagion** occurs when the experience of the same emotion

_____.

B. Feelings and Moods

1. Emotions, feelings, and moods are not the same.

2. **Feelings** are_____

_____.

3. **Moods** are_____

_____.

a. Moods powerfully influence our _____ and

_____.

b. One of the best ways to elevate your mood is through

_____.

C. Types of Emotions

1. Through examining patterns of _____,

_____, and _____, we can distinguish

among different types of emotions.

2. Scholars have identified six _____ emotions that involve _____ and

_____ behavioral displays across cultures.

3. These six emotions are _____,

_____, _____,

_____, _____, and

_____.

4. A **blended emotion** occurs when an event _____

_____.

II. Forces Shaping Emotion

A. Culture

1. In all cultures, **display rules** govern which forms of emotion management and

communication are _____ and _____.

2. Because of differences in _____,

_____, and _____, display rules show

considerable variation across cultures.

3. Skilled interpersonal communicators adjust their _____

_____ according to

_____.

B. Gender

1. Across cultures, women report experiencing more _____,

_____, _____, and

_____ than men, while men report feeling more

_____ and _____.

2. When men and women experience the same emotion, there is no difference in _____

_____.

C. Personality

1. Three of the "Big Five" personality traits strongly influence our experience and

communication of emotion. They are _____,

_____, and _____.

2. Albert Ellis developed _____ as a way for therapists to

help neurotic patients systematically purge themselves of self-defeating beliefs.

3. Personality is merely one of the many pieces that make up

_____.

III. Managing Your Emotional Experience and Expression

A. Emotional Intelligence

1. Emotional intelligence is defined as _____

_____.

2. People with high emotional intelligence possess these four skills:

_____, _____,

_____, and

_____.

3. **Emotion management** involves attempts to influence

_____,

_____, and

_____.

B. Managing Your Emotions after They Occur

1. One strategy for managing emotions is to try to

_____ or _____ them after we become aware of them.

2. **Suppression** involves_____

_____.

3. **Venting** is the inverse of suppression, and it means to_____

_____.

C. Preventing Emotions

1. An alternative to managing emotions is to

_____.

2. There are four strategies for preventing emotions:

a. **Encounter avoidance** involves_____

_____.

b. **Encounter structuring** is intentionally _____

_____.

c. **Attention focus** is devoting your attention to _____

_____.

d. **Deactivation** is systematically _____

_____ to emotional experience.

D. Reappraising Your Emotions

1. **Reappraisal** means actively changing

_____

so that their emotional impact is changed.

2. Reappraisal is effective because you employ it *before*

_____.

3. Reappraisal is accomplished in two steps.

a. First, call to mind_____.

b. Second, consider the_____

of your actions.

IV. Emotional Challenges

A. Some common emotional challenges are_____, _____,

_____, and _____.

1. Often, online encounters featuring the inappropriate expression of emotions result in

messages that _____ face-to-face.

a. We often communicate *asynchronously* online, which means we don't interact

   _____.

b. The *invisibility* of online communication can lead us to feel as if

   _____.

c. Without the ability to perceive others' immediate responses to our communication,

   it's difficult for us to experience _____

   and to _____.

   (i) We're less able to _____.

   (ii) We're less able to feel _____.

d. Three ways to express emotion more effectively online are:

   (i) Compensate for the empathy deficits by

        _____.

   (ii) Communicate these aspects of empathy by

        _____,

        _____,

        _____, and

        _____.

   (iii) Expect and be _____ of any potentially aggressive messages

        you receive, accepting that such behavior is the natural outcome of the online

        environment.

2. Anger

    a. **Anger** is a primary emotion that occurs when

    _____

    _____.

    b. The most frequently used strategy for managing anger is_____.

    c. **Chronic hostility** is caused by always

    _____ and is a near-constant state of

    _____.

    d. Another strategy for managing anger is _____.

        (i)   The concept of **catharsis** holds that_____

        _____.

        (ii) Venting provides a temporary sense of pleasure, but it actually

        _____.

        (iii) The _____ involves counting slowly to 10 before reacting

        to something that makes you angry.

3. **Passion** is a blended emotion that combines _____ and

    _____.

    a. The longer and better you know someone, the less passion you will experience

    toward him or her on a daily basis because_____

    _____.

    b. When it comes to passion, the best you can hope for in a long-term romantic

    relationship is _____.

4. **Grief** is the intense sadness that follows _____.

    a. To manage grief, you must use _____.

    b. When a person uses suppression to manage grief, he or she can end up experiencing

    _____

    _____.

    c. The best way to help others manage their grief is to engage in _____

    _____.

        (i) Amanda Holmstrom offers seven suggestions for improving your supportive communication:

           (a) Make sure the person is _____.

           (b) Find the right _____ and _____.

           (c) Ask _____.

           (d) _____, don't _____.

           (e) Listen _____.

           (f) _____ cautiously.

           (g) Show _____ and give _____.

V. Living a Happy Emotional Life

    A. Across all of our experiences, what balances our anger and grief is our

    _____.

    B. Our personal joy and happiness are determined by the quality of our

    _____.

WORD SEARCH

Each of the following clues is a key term from Chapter 4. Write the term in the space provided, and then find it hidden in the word search.

1. When her dog died, Jordan was overcome with intense sadness. This emotion is known as

   _____.

2. Violet and Rex have just started dating. When they're together, Violet feels excitement and

   joy, and every day they spend together is new and exciting. The blended emotion she feels is

   _____.

3. For months, Aylin was bothered by the way Sait interrupted her while she was talking. So, when

   Sait interrupted Aylin once again while she was telling a story, Aylin blew up at him, yelling

   and cursing. This explosive way of expressing emotion is known as _____.

4. Natalie had been attracted to Rayna since high school, but since Natalie had been taught that

   homosexuality was wrong, she inhibited her thoughts and displays of emotion. This is an

   example of _____.

5. Sandiq was kept up all night by his newborn baby. At his early morning meeting the next

   day, he was grouchy and irritable. The low-intensity state that Sandiq is in is called a(n)

   _____.

6. Isaiah is at a picnic when someone yells out that there is a swarm of bees near the playground.

   Soon all of the parents and picnic-goers are in a panicked frenzy to retrieve their children

   from the area. This rapid spreading of emotion from one person to another is called emotional

   _____.

7. Tannis is going through some old boxes when she finds her old cheerleading uniform. A wave

   of nostalgia and sentimentality washes over her. This short-term emotional reaction is called

   a(n) _____.

8. After breaking up with Darcy, Joe avoids the restaurant where they first kissed, the dry cleaner where she used to take his shirts, and the movie theater where they went every Thursday. Joe is using _____ avoidance as a strategy for preventing emotion.

```
G Z J E V G Q H J L V F T Y W L O Y C I L Z
C C T F H H J W Q I I F E N J C E K S Q D A
T D B N X A V D G M E Z O E K G J G O K K W
Q Q N I X T Q W S G L I P M L M J E Z Q C Q
X I E M M F U B S A S D Y L S I P B Z Z M L
U X Z U Q V B A R S U E Z D T R N Q Y J V H
V B V J N P A I A Z P U A E M Y M G G F B J
G M V V X O Y P Q A O G E G Q M Y L U G R X
O U W Z N I I H V T Q I B O O X D U A J X M
K Z Z W T A A G I S D U Z O D T R O G Z U Y
P P Y S Z N O F A X A L D L I K E Q F K F E
T R Y O B M R H I T H N R U U C T A V V W J
X N G F V Q T I R U N J O D D L N E S B O H
V E N T I N G O M Y L O C W V U U L D M A Q
F S B G H X Q L B R H Z C J J N O O Z N H S
N O I S S E R P P U S G Q R S I C N F Z C P
V Q U S Z Y X M O Q N R S C X M N W U M U A
H G F Z E U F I F M B I K M O G E T Z S C L
H R R J R G Y T I M D E X V B P A D O A X E
P Q Z F S X V I B H Q F F R T M I R E L Y K
H F R L R S E E F H A A N W A Z W M Q C E B
P I L M Y W H F K T K Y T K U G U P K X P F
```

DEFINING KEY TERMS

Write a sentence that defines each of the following key terms.

1. Emotion-sharing _____

_____

2. Catharsis _____

_____

3. Blended emotions _____

_____

4. Display rules _____

_____

5. Emotional intelligence _____

    _____

6. Emotion management _____

    _____

7. Deactivation _____

    _____

8. Encounter structuring_____

    _____

9. Attention focus _____

    _____

10. Chronic hostility _____

    _____

11. The Jefferson strategy _____

    _____

12. Supportive communication _____

    _____

CASE STUDY

Read and analyze the following case study, and then answer the questions regarding the nature of emotion and managing your emotional experience and expression.

Alina has a new roommate, Tyson. The weekend Tyson moves in, he has five friends over to watch "The Ultimate Fighting Championship." Alina is uncomfortable with the sport and does not appreciate the mess and noise that Tyson and his friends are making. She decides not to say anything to Tyson about her feelings because she does not want to get into a confrontation. The next day, Alina arrives home from work to find Tyson's friends at the house again. They continue to be loud, make a mess, and this time, they eat her groceries. Alina goes to a friend's house because she doesn't want to deal with Tyson and his friends. When she later comes home, the house is a complete disaster. She charges into Tyson's room, yelling at the top of her lungs. Naturally, a fight ensues.

1. What is the first strategy that Alina tries to use to manage her emotions?

2. What is the second strategy that Alina tries to use to manage her emotions? What effect does this have on the ultimate outcome of the situation?

3. How could Alina have managed her emotions better? What strategies might she utilize the next time Tyson's friends irritate her?

4. What effect might Alina's emotional strategies have on Tyson? What emotions might Tyson be experiencing toward Alina?

5. How could Alina apply the strategy of reappraisal to the described scenario?

SELF-TEST

For each of the following sentences, circle T if the statement is true or F if the statement is false.

T   F   1. Emotions occur many more times a day than feelings.

T   F   2. Kimberly sends an e-mail to coworkers stating only "THIS IS NOT MY JOB, IT'S YOURS!" She is not likely to say this in a face-to-face encounter.

T F 3. Display rules teach us what is culturally acceptable emotional communication.

T F 4. Catharsis is a persistent state of simmering anger.

T F 5. Gloria feels surprise and joy when she learns that she'll be a grandmother. These are examples of primary emotions.

T F 6. Grief is intense sadness that follows a substantial loss.

T F 7. The children are fighting in the back of the car, so Theo tries to concentrate even harder on the road. This is an example of attention focus.

T F 8. Teba can't stand her neighbor Trisha, so Teba never goes outside when she knows Trisha is there. This is an example of encounter structuring.

T F 9. Craig accidentally let Gerald's dog out of the house, and the dog ran away. Gerald counts to 100 before reacting to the news. This is an example of the Jefferson strategy.

T F 10. Carmen and Virginia are sitting in a coffee shop talking about work. This is an example of venting.

T F 11. Suppression is "bottling in" feelings or censoring outward displays of emotion.

T F 12. Anger is usually triggered by someone or something we perceive as improper or unfair.

T F 13. Laura bursts into the room excitedly—she is getting married today! This creates an excited "buzz" in the room. This is an example of emotional contagion.

T F 14. The two most common ways people manage their emotions are through suppression and venting.

T F 15. Reappraisal is actively changing how you think about the meaning of emotion-eliciting situations so that their emotional impact is changed.

T F 16. Deactivating is avoiding emotion-eliciting situations.

T F 17. Grief tends to linger for an extended amount of time compared to anger.

T F 18. Online support groups are viable alternatives to face-to-face support groups.

T F 19. The invisibility of online communication makes us feel as though we can't be seen or heard.

T F 20. Moods like boredom, contentment, or grouchiness are not caused by particular events.

JOURNAL ENTRY

Think of a time when you had to comfort another person who was experiencing grief. Did you use any of the seven suggestions for improving supportive communication listed in the text? Could you have improved your supportive communication? If yes, how?

_____

_____

_____

_____

_____

_____

_____

_____

_____

_____

_____

_____

_____

_____

_____

_____

_____

_____

_____

STUDY OUTLINE

Fill in the blanks to complete the outline.

I. Basics of Listening

    A. **Listening** is a _____ process that involves _____,

        _____, _____, _____, and

        _____.

    B. Rather than being instantaneous, the process of listening _____.

II. Listening: A Five-Step Process

    A. Receiving

        1. Together, _____ and _____ constitute **receiving**.

        2. Our ability to receive is often hampered by _____.

        3. The restricted ability to receive sound input across the humanly audible frequency range

           is called _____.

    B. Attending

        1. **Attending** involves _____ to the information you've received.

2. The extent to which you attend to received information is largely determined by its ___

_____.

3. We control our _____ level in two ways:

_____ and _____.

   a. Multitasking online involves using _____

_____.

     (i) Multitasking erodes your capacity for

_____.

     (ii) The effect known as *brain plasticity* explains why our brains

_____.

   b. Elevating attention requires five steps.

     (i) First, develop _____.

     (ii) Second, take note of encounters in which you *should* listen carefully, but that

       seem to _____.

     (iii) Third, consider the _____ of attention required

       for _____ during these encounters.

     (iv) Fourth, compare the _____ versus the

       level of attention that is _____.

     (v) Most importantly, _____ to the point

       necessary to take in the _____ and _____

       information you are receiving.

  c. _____ involves systematically putting aside thoughts that

aren't relevant to the interaction at hand.

C. Understanding

    1. **Understanding** involves _____

       by comparing _____

       _____.

    2. **Short-term memory** is where you place

       _____.

    3. **Long-term memory** is the part of your mind devoted to

       _____.

D. Responding

    1. **Responding** is communicating _____ and _____.

    2. **Feedback** comprises verbal and nonverbal behaviors used to communicate

      understanding and attention while _____.

      a. _____ are verbal and nonverbal behaviors such as nodding and

        making comments like "That makes sense."

      b. To effectively display positive feedback, you should make your feedback

        _____, _____, _____,

        and provide feedback _____.

    3. Active listeners communicate attention and understanding after the other person is done

      speaking.

      a. **Paraphrasing** is_____.

      b. Paraphrasing should be coupled with _____

        that take the conversation in new directions.

E. Recalling

   1. **Recalling** is _____.

   2. Recall accuracy varies _____.

   3. You can enhance your recall ability by using _____, devices that aid memory.

   4. The _____ causes us to remember unusual information more readily than commonplace information.

III. The Five Functions of Listening

A. The purposes for listening we experience daily are called _____.

B. Listening to comprehend means that you work to _____ the information that you receive.

C. Listening to discern means focusing on _____ _____.

D. When listening to analyze, you carefully evaluate the message you're receiving and you _____ it.

E. When listening to appreciate, your goal is simply to_____ _____.

F. Listening to support involves providing _____ to a conversational partner.

G. The five **listening functions** are not mutually _____, which means we _____ frequently and fluidly.

IV. Understanding Listening Styles

    A. Your **listening style** is your habitual pattern of listening behaviors, which

reflects your _____, _____, and

_____.

        1. **Action-oriented** listeners want _____

            _____.

        2. **Time-oriented** listeners prefer _____ encounters.

        3. **People-oriented** listeners view listening as_____

            _____.

        4. **Content-oriented** listeners prefer to be_____

            _____.

        5. To be an active listener, you must use_____ so you can

            _____.

    B. Women and men consistently differ in their listening style preferences and practices.

        1. Women are more likely than men to use _____ and

            _____ listening styles.

        2. Men tend to use _____ and _____listening

        styles.

    C. What is considered effective listening by one culture is often perceived as

    _____ by others.

        1. _____ and _____ listening styles are dominant in

        individualistic cultures, such as_____.

2. _____ and _____ listening styles are more

common in collectivist cultures.

V. Preventing Incompetent Listening

    A. **Selective listening** means taking in only _____

_____ during an interpersonal

encounter and_____the rest.

    B. **Eavesdropping** occurs when people intentionally and systematically

_____.

    C. **Pseudo-listening** means behaving _____

_____.

    D. **Aggressive listening**, also called _____, is attending to what others say solely

to _____.

    E. People who post online messages for the purpose of triggering attacks are called

_____.

    F. **Narcissistic listening** is self-absorbed listening during which the person ignores what

others have to say and _____.

VI. The Gift of Active Listening

    A. We surmount the challenges of active listening when we

_____, _____,

_____, and _____.

WORD SEARCH

Each of the following clues is a key term from Chapter 5. Write the term in the space provided, and then find it hidden in the word search.

1. Lorelei is watching the news and waiting for the traffic report. When it comes on, she consciously focuses her attention on the television. This is an example of_____.

2. Kaveh's mother tells him to stand up straight and tuck in his shirt. In response, Kaveh rolls his eyes. His response is an example of _____.

3. Miguel remembers the names of all of his grandchildren. This information is stored in his _____ memory.

4. The prefixes in the metric system can be remembered using the following saying: King Henry Died Monday Drinking Chocolate Milk (Kilo-, Hecto-, Deca-, Main unit, Deci-, Centi-, Milli-). This is an example of a(n) _____.

5. While speaking on the phone, Darren told his girlfriend, Bituin, that he was listening to her, even though he was actually checking his e-mail. This is a form of _____ listening.

6. Tang asks Donella to tell her all about Donella's family trip to Europe because she enjoys hearing about Donella's experiences with the food, culture, and art. Tang is a(n) _____-oriented listener.

7. Kim repeated his number several times, but Autumn just couldn't remember it. Autumn is experiencing difficulty with the _____ stage of the listening process.

8. Yumiko's mother asks her to do three things: put the laundry in the dryer, start the dishwasher, and pick up a chocolate cake for dessert. Yumiko listens and responds only to the message about chocolate cake because it's her favorite food. This is an example of _____ listening.

```
X D F V R L Y T G L Q F E D Q I K L W M E P
I D Z N R B T N Y M E M Z T C N I V I T L R
U M J C E B I W C E Y M L E Q I Z Q T T P K
G M B D L D Z R D R I D L R S X N W D S O V
M T B O N X U B E M R E T G N O L O E E E W
M Y C E C C A M R C A M X X Z X H F M L P B
X S T U Z C L E I X A G K B N F J W L E M M
U T Z J K T R V S K D L K K L V B J A C N W
A V N G M K B F Z Z F F L A A V H A P T T M
A V L U M S Z Q P P X M O I L O F Q Z I B P
D R H Z W Z J E J Q F I W N N P K G O V A T
J W K Y K J K S V G R L G D R G T V E E F D
S P D H U E D F S O V Y F C I J O O S E J R
B J O E K Q S A K L L T Q U J F U W X Q Q I
S R L K C Y S T V R Y X D U V V Y Y R R O B
Z Z C B J Z W S S C J A O T A K S Q S R D U
Y V E L D H V N K L B M B Q H O R K J S M L
A J W Z X N A L R C F T Q U N Q Q Z S I D D
Q K K D L X H I O W X D F U U W F P E O V V
P L A X S J V X J N G K Z N X P B Q O Q B K
J L L E O K Z J P R L P E J I G T M X E G M
A M B U S H I N G R U Z R V H Z N C E G F Y
```

DEFINING KEY TERMS

Write a sentence that defines each of the following key terms.

1. Mental bracketing _____

   _____

2. Short-term memory _____

   _____

3. Back-channel cues _____

   _____

4. Bizarreness effect _____

   _____

5. Listening functions _____

   _____

6. Action-oriented listeners _____

   _____

7. Time-oriented listeners _____

_____

8. Provocateurs _____

_____

9. Content-oriented listeners _____

_____

10. Selective listening _____

_____

11. Aggressive listening _____

_____

12. Narcissistic listening _____

_____

CASE STUDY

Read and analyze the following case study, and then answer the questions regarding active listening.

Thirteen-year-old Isabella is unhappy because a boy she likes at school doesn't seem to notice her. Isabella's mother, Leigh, sees that Isabella is upset and asks her what's wrong. Isabella explains the situation. Leigh immediately responds that Isabella is much too young to be interested in boys and that fraternizing with the opposite gender is inappropriate. This just makes Isabella more upset, and she says that Leigh never listens to her. Leigh immediately begins giving Isabella advice on love and relationships. Isabella sighs and nods, pretending to listen, even though she doesn't really want the advice.

1. At the beginning of the scenario, what type of listening is Leigh exemplifying?

2. Why does Leigh's initial response upset Isabella even further?

3. If Leigh listens in order to analyze with Isabella, what is likely to happen in future communication interactions between them?

4. Why doesn't Isabella want to hear the relationship advice? What type of listening would be most effective in this scenario?

5. What type of ineffective listening behavior does Isabella exhibit?

SELF-TEST

For each of the following sentences, circle T if the statement is true or F if the statement is false.

T F 1. Employees at fast-food restaurants often use an action-oriented listening style.

T F 2. When a lawyer cross-examines a witness and is looking for discrepancies in his or her testimony, the lawyer is engaged in aggressive listening.

T F 3. Hearing is the same as attending.

T F 4. Giving a "thumbs up" signal after your boss asks you how it's going is an example of a back-channel cue.

T F 5. We are less likely to remember information if it is odd or unusual.

T   F   6. Content-oriented listeners prefer to hear messages with a lot of emotional connections.

T   F   7. Eavesdropping can occur accidentally.

T   F   8. Thelma gives Gene flowers with a message that says, "Thinking of you." Gene responds by giving her a warm embrace. The embrace is an example of feedback.

T   F   9. Hearing and listening are the same thing.

T   F   10. Multitasking online often helps a person improve his or her attention span.

T   F   11. Memories of your first trip to Disneyland at age 6 would be stored in your long-term memory.

T   F   12. Mental bracketing leads to ineffective listening.

T   F   13. "My Very Educated Mother Just Served Us Noodles" is an example of a mnemonic device used to remember the planets in our solar system.

T   F   14. When talking with her friends, Heidi keeps changing the topic so that she is the center of the conversation. This is an example of narcissistic listening.

T   F   15. Every day, Melissa asks her son Adam what he did in school that day. Melissa believes this habit strengthens her relationship with her son. In this example, Melissa is a people-oriented listener.

T   F   16. Provocateurs enjoy encouraging others to share emotional experiences in online chat-rooms.

T   F   17. If you've forgotten where you left your mobile phone, you've had a lapse in your short-term memory.

T   F   18. When Lily knocks on Professor Knight's door to ask a question, the professor says, "Make it quick—my office hours end in five minutes." This is an example of a time-oriented listener.

T   F   19. James's dad says, "Son, after you clean your room and eat lunch, you can have some ice cream." All James focuses on is the part where his dad mentions "ice cream." This is the recalling stage of the listening process.

T   F   20. Seeing is a sensory process that is essential to the receiving step of the listening process.

JOURNAL ENTRY

Describe a time when someone practiced ineffective listening behavior while you were trying to communicate with him or her. Define the ineffective listening method he or she used. How did you react? Did it cause a conflict to occur? How did this occurrence affect your relationship with the other party?

_____

_____

_____

_____

_____

_____

_____

_____

_____

_____

_____

_____

_____

_____

_____

_____

_____

_____

_____

Name: _____

Class: _____

Date: _____

STUDY OUTLINE

Fill in the blanks to complete the outline.

I. Characteristics of Verbal Communication

A. **Verbal communication** is the exchange of _____

_____ .

B. Language has five fundamental characteristics:

1. Language is _____, meaning that all languages are basically

giant collections of _____ in the form of words that allow us to

communicate.

2. Language is governed by _____ .

a. _____ rules tell us which words represent which objects.

b. _____ rules represent the do's and don'ts controlling

language, and these rules guide everything from _____ to

_____ to _____ .

3. Language is flexible.

   a. **Personal idioms** are words and phrases that have _____ within

   relationships.

   b. When large groups of people share creative variations on language rules, those

   variations are called _____.

4. Language is cultural in that language is the set of _____

   that members of a culture create to communicate their _____,

   _____, _____, and _____ with

   one another.

   a. In **high-context cultures**, people presume that listeners _____.

   b. In **low-context cultures**, people tailor their verbal communication to be

   _____, _____, and _____.

5. Language evolves: it constantly _____ as people add new words

   and phrases to their language and discard old ones.

II. Functions of Verbal Communication

   A. Verbal communication enables us to share _____ with others

   during _____.

   1. _____ is the literal meaning of words, agreed upon by members

   of a culture.

   2. _____ refers to additional understandings of a word's meaning

   based on the situation and the knowledge we and our communication partners share.

   B. Verbal communication shapes our _____ and our

   _____.

1. The view that language defines the boundaries of our thinking is known as

   _____.

2. The idea that people from different cultures perceive and think about the

   world in very different ways because language determines thought is known as

   _____.

C. **Naming** is creating _____ for objects.

D. Verbal communication enables us to perform actions with language, known as

   _____.

   1. The five types of speech acts are _____,_____,

      _____,_____, and

      _____.

E. Language happens within conversations.

   1. Conversations are _____, in that at least two people must

      participate in talk exchange.

   2. Conversations are _____ managed, and the people having

      the conversation decide who gets to _____, and for

      _____, each time they exchange turns.

   3. Conversation is _____, because conversation forms the foundation for

      _____ and for

      _____ generally.

   4. Conversations often adhere to *scripts*, which are _____

      _____.

F. Helping us manage our _____ is arguably the most profound

   function of verbal communication.

III. Cooperative Verbal Communication

    A. **Cooperative verbal communication** means that you produce messages that others can

       easily _____, that you take _____

       _____ for what you're saying, and that others feel

       _____.

    B. To produce understandable messages, we must abide by the _____.

       1. Being informative means presenting _____

          _____, and it means avoiding being

          _____.

       2. The single most important characteristic of cooperative verbal communication is

          _____.

       3. Being relevant means making your conversational contributions

          _____.

       4. Be clear by presenting information in a _____, rather than framing

          it in obscure or ambiguous terms.

       5. **Misunderstanding** occurs when one person misperceives another's thoughts,

          feelings, or beliefs as expressed in the other individual's _____

          _____.

          a. Failure to _____ is a common cause of misunderstanding.

          b. Misunderstandings occur frequently online, owing to the lack of

             _____ cues to help clarify meaning.

          c. If a particular message absolutely must be error-free or if its content is controversial,

             don't use _____ or _____ to communicate it.

C. **"I" language** involves the use of phrases that emphasize _____

of your _____, _____, and

_____.

    1. Conversely, _____ involves phrases that place the focus of attention

    and blame on other people.

    2. Wordings that emphasize inclusion are known as _____.

D. When it comes to men's and women's verbal communication styles, research suggests that

_____

_____.

E. Culture exerts a _____ on verbal communication.

    1. **Communication accommodation theory** states that people are especially motivated to

    _____ when they seek

    _____, when they wish to

    _____, and when they view

    _____.

    2. Research suggests that when you _____ adjust your language use to

    match that of others from different cultures, you will be perceived as

    _____.

IV. Barriers to Cooperative Verbal Communication

A. **Communication apprehension** is _____

_____.

    1. Overcoming communication apprehension is possible by developing

    communication_____, which are

    _____.

a. The first part of a communication plan is _____, the

_____ in an encounter that

causes you anxiety.

b. The second part is _____, the messages

_____ and

_____.

B. **Defensive communication** is a second barrier to cooperative verbal communication,

comprising impolite messages delivered in response to _____,

_____, or _____.

1. Four common types of defensive communication are _____ messages,

_____ messages, _____ messages, and

_____ messages.

2. Defensive communication is _____, because it violates

_____, rarely succeeds in

_____, and treats others with

_____.

C. **Verbal aggression** is the tendency to _____

_____.

D. **Deception** occurs when _____

_____.

1. _____ involves leaving important and relevant information out of

messages.

2. Deception is _____, _____,

_____, and _____.

V. The Power of Verbal Communication

    A. The power of language is intensely _____.

    B. The words we exchange profoundly affect not only our interpersonal communication and

        relationships but also _____.

WORD SEARCH

Each of the following clues is a key term from Chapter 6. Write the term in the space provided, and then find it hidden in the word search.

1. While selling Mary a used car, Jesse omitted the fact that the car had been in a flood and three

    accidents. Intentionally omitting these important details is an example of _____.

2. William tells the Girl Scout who comes to his door selling cookies, "Sorry, I would buy some

    but I don't have any money." This direct and clear manner of speaking is characteristic of

    _____ cultures.

3. Manolo and Hailee call each other "love bug." This is an example of a personal

    _____.

4. Christina asks Marie, "Have you eaten dinner yet?" and Marie responds, "No. What do you feel

    like tonight?" These discrete units of conversation are known as _____.

5. Naveen tells the engineering team, "You guys just can't seem to pull it together before

    the deadline! You need to concentrate and stop messing around!" This accusatory style of

    communication is called _____ language.

6. The word *can* has several meanings: it is a metal vessel for storing food, it refers to the

    ability to do something, and it is also slang for getting terminated from a job. These are all

    _____ meanings.

7. Julia told Roy to pick her up outside the bar. Roy waited outside the side entrance to the bar, while Julia was out front. This is an example of a(n) _____.

8. In Roman numerals, *I* represents "one," *II* represents "two," and so forth. Roman numerals are an example of _____.

```
L M A D S J M L U H M O E V W O G Z R S E E
F U D E F B M P M W T G M D E I O P C X A U
E A T N F N A S T L K G Q T A D A X E B D C
C A H P W X G R V X I N E I R U S V J X I T
M I S U N D E R S T A N D I N G P I D S T C
L Q U X W C J F V D W K P N L A E D C K E L
Z O P L K U E A E F L K V I P M E G H F M V
B O W U G F N Q O C O Y T E K C L P X U X
M M H C V X O H G D R C N J A Z H H A K D H
A U C C O T P H S I W K S R E V A V N C M L
A V E B A N H Z Y L L L T F X G C Z S I Q L
Z U T T R P T I D R O M A F F N T B X I L S
Y H I R U U B E U N O B X Q Z K S U H K B E
A V R D Q C M X X E F J M Y F V I Q R F K C
E E C T K T G R T T R W E Y K M I H U H W D
F L N L V A M I Z J D O U O S O F V Y R K S
A H G M Z W F Q U Z W C H B S I H R F V W Q
L X I H U X V B Y T Z P M T G D F S V Y R C
X H B O R D Z H I F W O C D Z I H W S T R W
S J Y L Z G N O I T P E C E D C H N S W D X
V A G W L Z F V G K M Q Z B G I A B H R P H
T Z E P G Q T I B B X O F X R X S K N J O D
```

DEFINING KEY TERMS

Write a sentence that defines each of the following key terms.

1. High-context cultures _____

_____

2. Connotative meanings _____

_____

3. Linguistic determinism _____

_____

4. Linguistic relativity _____

_____

5. Cooperative verbal communication _____

_____

6. Cooperative Principle _____

_____

7. Communication accommodation theory _____

_____

8. Communication apprehension _____

_____

9. Naming _____

_____

10. Deception _____

_____

11. Constitutive rules _____

_____

12. Communication plan _____

_____

CASE STUDY

Read and analyze the following case study, and then answer the questions regarding cooperative verbal communication and misunderstanding.

Ashley and Arthur have been dating for two years. Last night as Arthur was walking out the door, he told Ashley, "I'll be back!" and waved over his shoulder. Now it's 7:30 a.m. and Ashley has been waiting up all night. Arthur finally walks in the front door with a nonchalant expression on his face. He smiles and greets Ashley with, "Good morning. You're up early." After seeing that he's not injured, Ashley exclaims, "Geez, Arthur! You didn't even call me! Where have you been? You inconsiderate jerk!" Arthur's facial expression changes immediately. He yells back, "It's none of your business where I've been! You're not my mother! I don't always have to report to you!" Ashley takes a deep breath and collects herself. She replies, "I was worried sick when you didn't call or come home. I called every hospital just to be sure you hadn't gotten into an accident." Arthur is still fuming. "Nobody asked you to look after me!" he yells. Ashley doesn't want to engage in further conflict, so she tells Arthur she's going for a walk. When she comes home two hours later, ready to talk it out, she finds a note from Arthur that simply reads, "I need some time away. I'm sorry." Ashley is sad and confused.

1. How is Arthur's message of "I'll be back!" an example of poor cooperative verbal communication?

2. What are some examples of "you" language in this scenario?

3. How does the use of "you" language escalate the conflict?

4. How is "I" language used in the scenario?

5. Do you think the cause of this argument is a misunderstanding, or something else?

SELF-TEST

For each of the following sentences, circle T if the statement is true or F if the statement is false.

T   F   1. An engagement ring is a symbol.

T   F   2. Kevin tells his girlfriend, "We need to be better at managing our finances." This is an example of a speech act.

T   F   3. The term *verbal communication* refers only to spoken language, not to written communication.

T   F   4. Kurt is talking to his new boss, Tony, for the first time. To make a favorable impression, Kurt adjusts his speech rate and clarity to match Tony's. This is an example of a constitutive rule.

T   F   5. The connotative meaning of a word is the dictionary definition or literal meaning.

T   F   6. Cooperative verbal communication means speaking in a clear, inclusive, and responsible way.

T   F   7. If you omit important details on purpose, you are being deceptive.

T   F   8. "Beating around the bush" and saying things in an indirect manner are characteristics of high-context cultures.

T   F   9. "I waited for over an hour, and you didn't even bother to call to tell me you were going to be late!" said Tabitha. This is an example of "I" language.

T   F   10. There are several different words for "waves" in Hawaiian, but in English, we only have one; therefore, English speakers have a limited way of perceiving waves compared to Hawaiian speakers. This is an example of linguistic relativity.

T   F   11. Carol experiences communication apprehension when it comes to confronting Andrew about leaving his dirty clothes on the floor. Making a communication plan can help her overcome her apprehension. .

T   F   12. When Jade was a baby, she used to make grunting and growling noises like a bear, so now, even as a teenager, her family members still call her Bear. This is an example of a personal idiom.

T   F   13. The idea that we talk one at a time as opposed to everyone talking at once is an example of a regulative rule.

T   F   14. One characteristic of language is that its constitutive rules may change but its regulative rules are constant.

T   F   15. Raul left a note on the refrigerator for Mona that read, "I left a slice of pie for you. Have a good day!" The note is an example of verbal communication.

T   F   16. Annabelle is presenting a speech in front of the city council. She purposefully leaves out statistics about the crime rate. This is an example of deception.

T   F   17. "I" language is the opposite of "we" language.

T   F   18. In Tagalog, the national language of the Philippines, *mahal* means both "love" and "expensive." This is an example of a dialect.

T   F   19. Even though people all over the world speak different languages, we all tend to perceive the world in a similar way.

T   F   20. Misunderstandings are always unintentional.

JOURNAL ENTRY

Write about a time when you experienced a misunderstanding. What was the cause of the misunderstanding (poor listening, relationship intimacy, misinterpretation)? What effects did it have on the situation or the relationship? Did it escalate into an argument? What can be done within the relationship to avoid misunderstanding in the same context in the future?

_____

_____

_____

_____

_____

_____

_____

_____

_____

_____

_____

_____

_____

_____

_____

_____

_____

_____

CHAPTER 7

*Communicating
Nonverbally*

Name: _____

Class: _____

Date: _____

STUDY OUTLINE

Fill in the blanks to complete the outline.

I. Principles of Nonverbal Communication

   A. **Nonverbal communication** is the intentional or unintentional transmission of meaning

   through _____

   _____.

   1. Nonverbal communication uses multiple _____ simultaneously, such as

   _____, _____, and _____.

   2. Nonverbal meanings are more _____ and _____ than

   verbal meanings.

   3. Nonverbal communication is governed by fewer _____ than verbal

   communication.

   4. Nonverbal communication has more _____ than verbal

   communication.

   a. Verbal and nonverbal behaviors that convey contradictory meanings are called

   _____.

B. Nonverbal communication and culture are _____ linked.

   1. The link between culture and nonverbal communication makes cross-cultural

     communication _____.

   2. Most people need _____

     before they fully understand the meanings of that culture's nonverbal communication.

C. Nonverbal communication is also influenced by _____.

   1. Although online content regarding interpersonal communication and relationships often

     is inaccurate and _____, some scholarship on nonverbal communication

     and gender is based on research.

     a. Psychologist Judith Hall's findings suggest four consistent patterns, the first of which

       states the following: women are better than men at both _____ and

       _____ nonverbal messages.

     b. Second, Hall's findings state that women show greater facial

       _____ than men.

     c. Third, Hall's findings state that women _____ at others during

       interpersonal interactions.

     d. Finally, Hall's findings state that men are more _____ than

       women.

D. As recently as 20 years ago, our ability to communicate nonverbally was radically

   restricted by_____, but now nonverbal communication has

   been _____.

   1. The first notable outcome of nonverbal technological liberation is that now we can

     choose _____.

2. The second outcome is that we can use these media to

_____.

E. Nonverbal and verbal expression _____ to create communication.

II. Nonverbal Communication Codes

A. **Nonverbal communication codes** are _____

_____.

B. _____ is the richest nonverbal code, because it includes visible

_____ such as facial expression, eye contact, gestures, and body

postures.

1. We use facial expression to communicate

_____ and we

make _____ about what others are feeling by assessing their facial

expressions.

2. We can use _____ to express emotions or to convey hostility.

a. One of the most aggressive forms of nonverbal expression is

_____.

3. **Gestures** take many forms.

a. **Emblems** represent _____, whereas

_____ accent or illustrate verbal messages.

b. **Regulators** control _____, whereas

adaptors are touching gestures that _____

_____.

4. **Posture** communicates both _____ and _____.

C. **Vocalics** are vocal _____ we use to communicate nonverbal

   messages.

   1. People's voices are complex combinations of four characteristics:

      _____, _____,

      _____, and _____.

   2. _____ involves a combination of _____ and

      _____.

   3. _____ refers to whether a voice is high or low.

   4. Emphasizing words, through increased volume in speech or CAPITAL LETTERS

      online, relates to _____.

   5. The speed at which you speak is called _____.

D. Communicating through touch is known as _____.

   1. Scholars distinguish between six types of touch: _____,

      _____ , _____,

      _____, _____, and

      _____.

E. Communicating through the use of physical distance is called

   _____.

   1. Intimate space ranges from _____ to _____ inches.

   2. _____ ranges between 18 inches and 4 feet.

   3. Social space ranges between _____ feet.

   4. _____ ranges upward from 12 feet.

5. _____ is the tendency to claim physical space as our own and to

    define certain locations we don't want others to invade without permission.

F. The way you use time to communicate during interpersonal encounters is called

    _____.

    1. People who have **M-time** orientation value _____

        _____.

    2. People who have **P-time** orientation value _____

        _____.

G. How you look conveys as much about you as what you say because we communicate

    through _____.

    1. Beauty counts, and one factor that's related to attractiveness across cultures is

        _____.

H. _____ are the things we possess that influence how we see ourselves and

    that we use to express our identity to others.

I. We communicate through our **environment**, the _____ of our

    surroundings; our environment includes both_____ features and

    _____ features.

III. Functions of Nonverbal Communication

A. We sometimes use nonverbal communication to _____ convey

    _____, like giving a thumbs-up to indicate a good job.

B. We use nonverbal communication more indirectly in five ways:

    1. To _____ verbal messages, such as pointing left and saying "Turn left

        here."

2. To _____ our verbal messages, such as saying we're not angry when we're scowling.

3. To _____ the meaning of verbal messages, such as holding a scared child close while telling him that he's safe.

4. To _____ verbal expressions altogether, such as simply nodding to communicate agreement.

5. To _____ certain parts of messages, such as saying one word more loudly than others: "STOP running by the pool."

C. _____ are intentional or unintentional behaviors that convey actual or feigned emotions.

D. Nonverbal communication can help us present different _____ of our _____ to others.

E. Nonverbal communication also helps us to _____ interpersonal interactions.

F. We use our nonverbal communication to create _____ and to define _____ or _____ in our relationships.

1. Nonverbal communication helps to create **intimacy**, which is a feeling of

_____

_____.

2. Nonverbal communication can also convey _____, the interpersonal behaviors we use to _____, and _____, the willingness to allow others to _____.

IV. Competently Managing Your Nonverbal Communication

    A. In interactions, you use various nonverbal communication codes naturally and

      _____.

    B. People view your nonverbal communication as _____ as what you

      say, if not _____.

    C. Nonverbal communication competence is inextricably tied to _____.

    D. Be sensitive to the demands of interpersonal situations and adapt your nonverbal

      communication _____.

    E. Remember that verbal communication and nonverbal communication _____

      _____.

WORD SEARCH

Each of the following clues is a key term from Chapter 7. Write the term in the space provided, and then find it hidden in the word search.

1. Domingo drives a Lexus, wears designer suits, and owns the biggest house on the block. These

   objects that he uses to influence how others view him are called _____.

2. Thomas is driving down the freeway when another driver cuts him off. Thomas rolls down his

   window and brandishes a fist at the other driver. This gesture that symbolizes anger is known as

   a(n) _____.

3. When Jeff starts talking, Rachelle sits up straight, stops what she is doing, and looks at him. The

   interest that Rachelle conveys through her body language is called _____.

4. Hienzel answers the telephone at work, "Financial Fitness Incorporated. I'll be happy to help

   you," with a bored, uninviting tone. This contradiction between her verbal and nonverbal

   communication is an example of a(n) _____ message.

5. Lani and the rest of her family decide that it's all right to be a little late to their cousin's party because they are enjoying the sun at the beach so much. This cultural orientation toward viewing time loosely is called _____.

6. Increasing your volume when speaking might signal anger or surprise, or it might help the other person hear more clearly. The nonverbal code that represents vocal characteristics is known as _____.

7. Solon holds her patient's arm while giving him a flu shot. This type of touch is known as _____-professional touch.

8. Nati and Tanisha are talking excitedly at a busy coffee shop about Tanisha's date that night. The proxemic zone they are most likely inhabiting is known as _____ space.

```
M D U K M O K D V V W F D S U M P C M Q Z H
S X A W D U H L P Z E U U R C K B E X K P R
Q T D R B M G Q O D W N B P O I L J U Y H G
C G W I Y X P J L W P C U W T B L P R E E G
Y P K V K S R N D N P T W G M I C A L X K A
R N T N W C B S D E M I V E W R M B C F P C
Y A Y C A I D E M M I O B I O A L E N O R F
D R D S L N G H X N N U M R A A U R A V U
K J N A B T S O E F E A B T Z Y N S L Y Y L
O X K J B M P B E V R L I P R K O X J H X S
K F O X N X R E C H K F R Y Y R S Z N W Q N
B Z Y R P Q S U N N A J X W O E R C T O K Y
Y J J B Q D J G X C B V P U B Y E C J T O F
I G F H J O E Q T P D X J V K P P G U X C W
U P H A N E J S I C D R F L N N W W H O X T
Y A T W A P P O K J R H L Y N O J W Q Z J M
I N G U Z D X P J P U D G P T O L B W B Q Q
W Z C R R I F D Z K H D K V V J W T T V T E
G F C V N Z H A Z A M V N L C R L T M W Z B
D R S R T K X M I X E D C W B Z W Q V S A T
D Z P U X P Q Q V N Z L G B V J C Y H B Z O
B D R T S W Z S T G J Z N H O A U K Q T Y I
```

DEFINING KEY TERMS

Write a sentence that defines each of the following key terms.

1. Nonverbal communication _____

   _____

2. Nonverbal communication codes _____

   _____

3. Power _____

   _____

4. Social-polite touch _____

   _____

5. Proxemics _____

   _____

6. Territoriality _____

   _____

7. M-time _____

   _____

8. Intimate space _____

   _____

9. Physical appearance _____

   _____

10. Affect displays _____

    _____

11. Dominance _____

    _____

12. Submissiveness _____

    _____

CASE STUDY

Read and analyze the following case study, and then answer the questions regarding nonverbal communication.

Max and Tito are sitting in the food court at the mall. They are talking about nothing of consequence when Max notices a group of boys standing a few yards away who keep looking at them, whispering to each other, and then laughing. Max and Tito make eye contact and Max nods his head toward the group of boys. Tito looks over and sees the group staring and laughing. Tito stares back at the group with a menacing scowl. One boy in the group turns around and points to a patch on his jacket that reads, "Tae Kwon Do Champion 2013" on it. Max and Tito look at the patch and look at each other, and both sarcastically chew their fingernails as if to mock the other boy. Then Max and Tito fall into a fit of laughter. The boy wearing the patch cracks his knuckles, and his group begins to walk over to where Max and Tito are sitting.

1. What do Max and Tito infer from the nonverbal communication expressed by the other group of boys?

2. What message does Max's eye contact to Tito convey? What is Max trying to communicate to his friend by nodding to the other group of boys?

3. What is Tito trying to communicate to the other boys by staring at them with a menacing scowl?

4. What are some of the channels of nonverbal communication displayed in this encounter?

5. In your opinion, based on the information in the textbook, are these communicators responsibly managing their nonverbal communication? Why or why not?

SELF-TEST

For each of the following sentences, circle T if the statement is true or F if the statement is false.

T F 1. Actions speak louder than words.

T F 2. The more intimate you are with someone, the more nonverbal communication you share.

T F 3. Kinesics is the study of eye contact and space.

T F 4. Alexis and Makayla walk with their arms around each other. This is an example of love-intimacy touch.

T F 5. Gwen tells Hale that she isn't interested in him, but she is always flirting with him. This is an example of a mixed message.

T F 6. Shea writes down all her appointments and is never late. This is an example of P-time orientation.

T F 7. According to the definition of personal space in the textbook, if someone is "invading your personal space," he or she is 6 inches or closer to you.

T F 8. You can exude power through physical appearance.

T F 9. Raising your hand in class is an example of a regulator.

T   F   10. Maricella wears Hector's jacket to show they are exclusively dating. This is an example of an affect display.

T   F   11. Alina owns expensive purses and shoes and drives a Mercedes-Benz. These are artifacts that may influence others to believe she is rich.

T   F   12. You can exert dominance over someone by using silence.

T   F   13. A fast-food restaurant's hard seats and harsh lighting are an example of how emblems can cause customers to eat quickly and leave right away.

T   F   14. Kyle, Chad, and Chase are at the movies. While Chad and Chase go to buy some popcorn, Kyle puts his coat over the other two seats to indicate that they're reserved. This is an example of territoriality.

T   F   15. Eli is giving Katie the silent treatment after they got into an argument the night before. Eli is using haptics to represent anger.

T   F   16. Jason has the habit of pulling his left ear while talking to people for the first time. This is an example of an adaptor.

T   F   17. June shakes her new coworker's hand. This is an example of functional-professional touch.

T   F   18. Increased eye contact, nodding, and smiling are all nonverbal ways to communicate immediacy.

T   F   19. The socially acceptable distance that we keep between ourselves and others during conversation varies from culture to culture.

T   F   20. Loudness, a characteristic of vocalics, can be adapted to online communication.

JOURNAL ENTRY

Which of the eight nonverbal communication codes are you most aware of using when meeting a potential friend for the first time? A potential romantic interest? Describe a recent interpersonal interaction when you reacted negatively to someone's nonverbal communication codes. Compare it with a time when you reacted positively to someone's nonverbal communication codes. What do these interactions tell you about your own cultural expectations for nonverbal communication?

STUDY OUTLINE

Fill in the blanks to complete the outline.

I. Conflict and Interpersonal Communication

    A. **Conflict** is the process that occurs when people perceive that they have

    _____ or that someone is interfering with

    _____.

        1. Conflict begins with _____.

        2. Conflict involves _____.

        3. Conflict is a _____ that unfolds

        _____.

        4. Conflict is _____, and most conflicts proceed through several

        _____.

            a. When a conflict shifts topic, it can devolve into **kitchen-sinking**, in which

            _____

            _____.

    B. Most conflicts occur between people who know each other and are involved in

    _____.

1. In close relationships, conflicts typically arise from _____,

   _____, and _____.

2. Relationship partners often develop consistent patterns of communication for dealing

   with conflict that either _____ or _____ their

   happiness.

3. Conflicts with loved ones are guaranteed to be _____ and

   _____ experiences.

4. Conflicts also powerfully affect your _____ encounters and

   relationships.

II. Power and Conflict

A. **Power** is the ability to _____ other people and events.

   1. Power is _____ present.

      a. Relationships with balanced power (e.g., friend to friend) are _____

         relationships, whereas those with imbalanced power (e.g. manager to employee) are

         _____ relationships.

   2. According to _____ , people with only

      _____ power are likely to use _____.

   3. Power can be used _____ or _____.

   4. Power is granted, meaning that individuals or groups allow another person or group to

      _____ over them.

   5. Power _____ conflicts.

B. In order to acquire power, you must possess or control some form of _____

   _____.

1. _____ currency includes material things such as money, property, food, and the like.

2. **Expertise currency** comprises _____

_____.

3. A person who is linked with a circle of friends, family, and acquaintances has

_____.

4. Examples of **personal currency** are _____

_____.

5. You acquire **intimacy currency** when _____

_____.

C. Views of power _____ across cultures.

1. The degree to which people view the unequal distribution of power as acceptable is

known as _____.

2. Within *high power-distance cultures*, people give privileged treatment and extreme

respect to those in _____.

3. In *low power-distance cultures*, people in high-status positions strive to

_____, often

_____.

D. Throughout history and across cultures, the defining distinction between the genders has

been _____.

1. Through patriarchy, men have used cultural practices to maintain their

_____, _____, and

_____ power.

2. Whereas men may feel satisfied that their voices are being heard in their relationships, women often feel as though their _____

_____, both at home and in the workplace.

III. Handling Conflict

    A. People generally handle conflict in one of five ways: _____,

_____, _____,

_____, and _____.

    B. Ignoring a conflict, pretending it isn't really happening, or communicating indirectly about the situation is called _____, which takes several forms:

      1. In **skirting**, a person _____ by

_____.

      2. _____ is communicating in a negative fashion and then

_____

_____.

      3. Avoidance is the _____ approach to handling conflict.

      4. One risk of using avoidance is _____, in which repressed irritation grows as the mental list of grievances we have against our partners builds.

      5. A second risk is _____, the perception that a conflict exists when

_____.

    C. Through **accommodation**, one person abandons _____

_____.

    D. _____ is an open and clear discussion of the goal clash that exists and the pursuit of one's own goals without regard for others' goals.

1. Competitive approaches can trigger _____ communication.

2. The primary risk of this approach is **escalation**, which is _____

_____.

E. Reactivity is characterized by accusations of _____,

_____, _____, and becoming

_____.

1. Reactivity is decidedly _____.

F. _____ is the most constructive approach to managing conflict.

1. Often, the result of using a collaborative approach is _____.

2. To use a collaborative approach, try these four suggestions from Wilmot and Hocker:

a. First, _____.

b. Second, _____.

c. Third, _____.

d. Finally, _____.

IV. The Influence of Gender, Culture, and Technology on Conflict

A. Traditional gender socialization creates challenges for _____ as they

seek to resolve conflicts.

1. Women are encouraged to avoid and suppress conflict and to sacrifice

_____.

2. Men, in contrast, learn to adopt _____ approaches to

interpersonal conflict.

3. Avoid assuming that no conflict exists just because the other person

_____.

B. Whether you belong to a(n) _____ culture or a(n)

_____ culture is the strongest cultural factor that

influences your conflict approach.

1. People raised in collectivist cultures often view direct messages regarding conflict as

_____.

2. People raised in individualistic cultures feel comfortable _____ to

_____.

C. Many conflicts occur through technology (e.g., e-mail, texting, Web posts, etc.).

Unfortunately, such media are not _____ for

_____. Thus, the most important step in managing conflict

constructively is to_____.

1. If you must deal with a conflict online, try these suggestions:

a. First, _____.

b. Second, _____.

c. Third, _____.

d. Fourth, _____.

e. Last, _____.

V. Conflict Endings

A. Short-term conflict resolutions take one of four forms:

1. The sudden withdrawal of one person from an encounter is called _____.

2. **Domination** occurs when _____

_____.

3. During _____, both parties change their goals to make them

compatible.

4. Through _____, the two sides preserve and attain their

goals by developing a creative solution to their problem.

5. In cases of especially intense conflict, _____, people

agreeing to change the basic rules or understandings that govern their relationship to

prevent further conflict, may result.

B. Research has found that certain approaches for dealing with conflict strongly predict

_____.

1. People who use _____ have lower relationship

satisfaction and endure longer and more frequent conflicts than people who don't

_____.

2. Collaborative approaches generally generate _____ outcomes.

VI. Challenges to Handling Conflict

A. The concept of self-enhancing thoughts suggests that individuals selectively

remember information that _____ and

_____ their partners.

1. People typically do not consider_____.

2. Instead, their thoughts are locked into _____,

_____, and _____ views.

3. To improve your conflict-management skills, routinely practice

_____ during disputes.

B. Destructive messages can permanently _____ our relationships.

1. **Sudden-death statements** occur when people get so angry they suddenly

   _____.

2. Perhaps the most destructive messages are_____, statements

   that are honest in content, but have been kept hidden to

   _____.

C. **Serial arguments** are a series of unresolved disputes, all having to do with _____

   _____.

1. Sometimes, one partner in a relationship demands that his or her goals be met, and the

   other partner responds by withdrawing from the encounter. This is known as a _____

   _____ pattern.

D. Physical violence is the most destructive conflict challenge.

1. Both men and women use violence as a strategy for dealing with conflicts, but women

   are substantially more likely to be injured or killed, owing to

   _____.

2. The _____ occurs when individuals stop discussing the

   relationship issues out of fear of their partners' negative reactions.

3. If you find yourself in a relationship with a partner who behaves violently, seek help

   from _____, _____, and, if necessary,

   _____.

E. Some disputes are _____.

1. One clue that a dispute is unsolvable is that you and the other person aren't

   _____ to change your _____ opinions of one

   another.

2. Another clue is that your goals are _____ and

   _____.

3. A final clue is that at least one partner is _____, _____

_____, or _____.

VII. Managing Conflict and Power

    A. Though conflicts carry risk, they also provide the opportunity to

        _____

        _____.

    B. The key distinguishing feature between conflict and power struggles that destroy and those that create opportunities for improvement is how you

        _____.

WORD SEARCH

Each of the following clues is a key term from Chapter 8. Write the term in the space provided, and then find it hidden in the word search.

1. When Samara saw Aidan at the grocery store, she immediately ducked behind a display of pasta sauce because she never repaid the $100 she borrowed from him a month ago. This way of handling conflict is called _____.

2. Aslan knows the bouncer at a very posh and elite nightclub. This kind of power is known as social _____ currency.

3. When Georgie and Kim were on the verge of breaking up, they instead went to counseling, completely changed the way they communicated, and redefined their roles in the relationship. These changes are called _____ improvements.

4. Celine confronts her coworker Dorian after work and angrily argues that he should not pursue a promotion that she thinks she deserves. Celine is engaging in _____ as a way of handling conflict while pursuing her own goals.

5. Jamie has been irritated with Lawrence for weeks. Lawrence never cleans up, always leaves dirty dishes in the kitchen, and doesn't put the groceries away. When he leaves the living room a mess one day, Jamie snipes at him, and a fight ensues. Jamie's built-up irritation grew into _____ annoyance.

6. When Cole and Miranda can't decide what kind of car to buy—a minivan or an SUV—Cole persuades Miranda that vans are safer, more practical, and more economical than her choice, an SUV, and Miranda gives in because Cole makes more money. Cole and Miranda's conflict was resolved through _____.

7. On a recent plane trip, Jacquie was the only doctor on board when a passenger had a heart attack. In this situation, Jacquie had _____ currency.

8. Marlon and Josh are fighting about whose turn it is to play video games. Josh bolts out of the room and goes outside to play basketball. This sudden withdrawal that results in short-term conflict resolution is called _____.

```
J I B Z K I V V W N G O J Z U L K H A S Z C
H V X X P C Q C O A V O I D A N C E B W O G
Q H R L S P J I X A U Y W F O Z B W Y M W S
O D M F D O T K J E X V T E Y G I E P A A J
L H H P W A V I O W H X I K M Z G E K O S F
F G P A R N G Z A L D S Y T I C T C N J D U
A I B A N E X R V S U K S Z L I I P P W K H
U U P S O O X W K E P A I Q T I R X M A D F
S E M R I D P P N U V Y D I I Q M G C L D N
S X D T T W N Q E J W I O L M H A K N T G Z
P P N E A J B E T R J N T L X L H T D S W H
D D O J N P X C W S T V K A D D D C M D N H
G Z Q G I R A A O T Q I E N L L B R B A Z B
M F I N M V E P R J T G S Y T U I R R U U W
Q S Z S O C M P K J W L B E X P M N K R J G
J O M M D A U Q B K M D W L G M C U E F I R
L A R U T C U R T S G U L E O P A T C G O I
K V I M M U X R O D N F G L T J Q B Y A T K
Z Y I Y W X T Y E J N S H H L A Z F U Z N P
Y U O K Y Z T V V Y F O M Q N Y Q J U R C I
D M J Q G K G I G Y Z I A T M J K J W U U K
D Z I U I M S K S C S U H M Y L M P O Y K Z
```

DEFINING KEY TERMS

Write a sentence that defines each of the following key terms.

1. Conflict _____

_____

2. Kitchen-sinking _____

_____

3. Power _____

_____

4. Complementary relationships _____

_____

5. Resource currency _____

_____

6. Power-distance _____

_____

7. Skirting _____

_____

8. Pseudo-conflict _____

_____

9. Accommodation _____

_____

10. Escalation _____

_____

11. Reactivity _____

_____

12. Integrative agreements _____

_____

CASE STUDY

Read and analyze the following case study, and then answer the questions regarding conflict and power in communication.

Matt and Christine are married and run a chiropractic practice together. Christine is the chiropractor, and Matt manages the office. At home, Matt and Christine make an extra effort to be fair, equal, and balanced in all aspects of their life, from housework to decision making. At work, they also try to make decisions together, but since Christine is the doctor, she often has the ultimate word in any disagreement. One day at work, Matt gets into a heated argument with a client over the phone. The client claims that he should not have to pay a bill because he never received an invoice. The client is being irrational and uncooperative. Matt tells the client that he is no longer welcome at their practice and hangs up on him. Christine is furious at Matt for being so unprofessional. At home that night, Matt asks Christine if she is mad at him and she says she isn't, but she is especially short with him, eats dinner without him, and sleeps in the spare bedroom. Matt does not want to argue with Christine, so he doesn't say anything about the cold way she is treating him.

1. Power is present in Matt and Christine's relationship in all contexts. Are Matt and Christine's positions of power within the household different from their positions of power in the workplace? How and why?

2. What types of power currencies does Christine have over Matt in the workplace? Does she have the same power currencies at home?

3. What type of conflict style does Matt exhibit with the client? What types of conflict style does he exhibit with Christine?

4. What types of conflict style does Christine exhibit with Matt?

5. Give an example of how both Matt and Christine can use a collaborative approach for managing conflicts.

SELF-TEST

For each of the following sentences, circle T if the statement is true or F if the statement is false.

T   F   1. Marcia is so tired of arguing with her roommate over who has to clean the bathroom, she just gives in and cleans it herself. This is an example of avoidance.

T   F   2. A key to using collaboration is to focus on common interests and long-term goals.

T   F   3. Competition involves confronting others.

T   F   4. An example of a complementary relationship is one between a boss and an employee.

T   F   5. Another term for a complementary relationship is a symmetrical relationship.

T   F   6. Sniping involves attacking a person and then eliminating the opportunity for him or her to respond.

T   F   7. When Sean yells, "Don't bother to ever call me again!" at his new girlfriend, this is an example of a sudden-death statement.

T   F   8. In a compromise, both parties must sacrifice their goals to some degree.

T   F   9. If a conflict begins online (via e-mail or another mediated channel), it should remain online.

T F 10. Chloe tells Nadine that her feelings are hurt by something Nadine said last night. Nadine immediately makes a joke about Chloe being too sensitive. This is an example of pseudo-conflict.

T F 11. Nina's husband is a famous football player. This gives her social network currency.

T F 12. At one time, Priscilla and Brent were both unhappy with the roles they played in their relationship. But then Brent decided to stay home to raise their sons while Priscilla took a high-paying job to support the family. Now they hardly ever fight about money or household chores. The changes Priscilla and Brent have made are called structural improvements.

T F 13. Power-distance means that the more power you are perceived to have, the farther away from you people tend to stand while communicating.

T F 14. Mea's mom takes away a toy every time Mea is naughty. The power that Mea's mom has is an example of resource currency.

T F 15. Competition, as a way of handling conflict, is generally healthy for a relationship.

T F 16. In close relationships, when a woman confronts a man during arguments, the man usually retreats. This is called the demand-withdraw pattern.

T F 17. Mike and Kate are arguing about Mike's staying out too late. Kate adds, "Not only do you stay out too late, you never help out with the kids, and you can't even wash your own dishes!" This is an example of kitchen-sinking.

T F 18. Dirty secrets are false accusations aimed at intentionally causing conflict.

T F 19. Joan and her friends are outside talking when Alex walks up to join the conversation. Just then, Joan walks away. Alex thinks Joan is angry with him, but in reality, Joan just doesn't like his cigarette smoke. This is an example of pseudo-conflict.

T F 20. An integrative agreement is based on collaboration.

JOURNAL ENTRY

The text describes how gender and culture typically affect the way an individual approaches conflict. Reflect on your own conflict-management style(s). To what extent do you think your gender and culture explain your personal style? In what ways? Cite some specific examples. What do you think are the greatest influences on how you've come to manage conflict in your life?

_____

_____

_____

_____

_____

_____

_____

_____

_____

_____

_____

_____

_____

_____

_____

_____

_____

_____

_____

STUDY OUTLINE

Fill in the blanks to complete the outline.

I. Defining Romantic Relationships

  A. _____ is a feeling of affection and respect.

    1. _____ is a sense of warmth and fondness for another person, while

      _____ is admiration for another person apart from how he or she

    treats you and communicates with you.

  B. In contrast _____ is a deeper and more intense

    emotional commitment that consists of three components: _____,

    _____, and _____.

  C. **Passionate love** is a state of _____

    _____.

    1. People in the throes of passionate love often view their loved ones and relationships

      _____.

    2. People from _____ feel passionate love.

    3. No _____ differences exist in people's experience of

    passionate love.

4. For adults, passionate love is integrally linked with _____ and

_____.

5. Passionate love is *negatively* related to

_____.

D. **Companionate love** is _____

_____.

E. The six **types of romantic love** are _____,

_____, _____,

_____, _____, and

_____.

F. A **romantic relationship** is a _____

_____, and it has six key

elements.

1. A romantic relationship exists whenever the two partners

_____.

2. Romantic relationships exhibit diversity in the _____

_____ of the partners, as well as their _____

and _____ backgrounds and _____

orientation.

3. We enter into romantic relationships through _____, selecting not only

with whom we _____ but also whether and how we

_____.

4. Romantic relationships often involve _____, a strong

psychological attachment to a partner and an intention to

_____.

a. Both men and women view commitment as a(n)

_____.

5. Within romantic relationships, we often experience competing impulses, or

_____, between our selves and our feelings toward others, known as

_____.

6. Romantic relationships are forged through

_____.

II. Romantic Attraction

A. Proximity, or being in one another's presence frequently, exerts far more impact on

_____ than many people think.

1. The **mere exposure effect** states that you will _____

_____

_____.

2. Proximity's effect on attraction is one reason that _____

_____

in the United States.

B. We view beautiful people as competent communicators, intelligent, and well adjusted, a

phenomenon known as the _____.

1. Our tendency to form long-term romantic relationships with people we judge as similar

to ourselves in physical attractiveness is known as _____.

C. The **birds-of-a-feather** effect suggests_____

_____.

D. **Reciprocal liking** is a potent predictor of attraction as we tend to be attracted to people

who are _____.

E. **Social exchange theory** proposes that people are drawn to those who offer

_____ with few _____.

F. The balance of benefits and costs exchanged within a relationship, known

as _____, determines whether the relationship will

_____.

    1. *Inequity*, which occurs when one person receives greater relationship benefits than the

       other person, creates partners who are _____ (they get more rewards

       for fewer costs) and partners who are _____ (they get fewer rewards

       for more costs).

G. Technology has refined and enhanced the attraction process.

    1. You can establish virtual proximity to attractive others by _____

       _____ and then

       _____.

    2. Because so many people now use online communication to gauge each other, you may

       feel great pressure to _____ as

       _____, even if doing so means providing a

       _____.

III. Relationship Development and Deterioration

A. Mark Knapp suggests that there are ten relational stages, starting with the five stages of

    "coming together."

    1. During the **initiating** stage, you _____

       _____.

    2. In the **experimenting** stage, _____

       _____.

a. Disclosing facts you and the other person consider relatively unimportant is called

_____.

b. Most relationships _____ beyond the experimenting stage.

3. In the **intensifying** stage, you and your partner begin to reveal

_____.

4. During the **integrating** stage, your and your partner's personalities

_____.

5. **Bonding** is a(n) _____ that announces your commitment to the

world.

B. Knapp describes five stages of "coming apart."

1. **Differentiating** is when the beliefs, attitudes, and values that distinguish you from your

partner come to _____

_____.

2. **Circumscribing** is characterized by actively _____

_____.

3. During the **stagnating** stage, both people presume that _____

_____.

4. In the **avoiding** stage, one or both of you decide that _____

_____, and you begin

_____.

5. The **terminating** stage involves a final encounter that

_____.

IV. Maintaining Romantic Relationships

    A. **Relational maintenance** refers to _____

      _____.

      1. Positivity includes communicating _____, doing

         _____, and

         _____.

      2. Assurances are messages that emphasize _____

         _____.

      3. Sharing tasks involves taking _____ and negotiating an

         _____.

      4. Acceptance involves communicating _____ and

         _____.

      5. To foster self-disclosure, each person must behave in ways that are

         _____, _____, and

         _____.

      6. _____ allow you to gauge how invested you each are

         and whether _____.

      7. Romances are more likely to _____ if important members of the

         couples' _____ approve of the relationship.

V. Maintaining Romance across Distance

    A. Contrary to popular belief, long-distance romantic relationships have actually been found

      to be _____ than those that are geographically close.

    B. The most difficult maintenance challenge long-distance couples face is not the separation,

      but their _____.

C. There are several suggestions to help maintain long-distance relationships:

    1. Use _____ to regularly communicate with your partner.

    2. Focus on maintenance tactics, particularly _____ and _____.

    3. Expect a significant period of _____ when you permanently reunite.

VI. Deciding Whether to Maintain

    A. Answering four questions can help predict the survival of a romance:

        1. _____?

        2. _____?

        3. _____?

        4. _____?

VII. The Dark Side of Romantic Relationships

    A. **Romantic betrayal** is defined as an act that _____ of a romantic

    relationship and, as a result, causes _____.

    1. Because betrayal is *intentional*, it evokes two intense, negative reactions:

        a. An overwhelming sense of _____.

        b. A profound sense of _____.

    2. _____ is the most destructive form of romantic betrayal.

    3. Deception involves misleading your partner by intentionally withholding

    _____, presenting _____, or making your message

    _____.

    4. The strongest predictor of what happens after a betrayal is the

    _____ of the betrayal.

B. **Jealousy** is a protective reaction to a _____

_____.

    1. Through **wedging**, a person deliberately uses messages, photos, and posts to try to

_____ because he or she is

_____.

    2. The most effective way to deal with jealousy is _____, which

means allowing yourself to feel jealous but not letting whatever sparked your jealousy

to _____ you.

C. The violation of one's independence and privacy by a person who desires an intimate

relationship is known as _____.

    1. One form of intrusion is _____, which might involve

persistent text messages inquiring about your whereabouts, or worse.

    2. A second form of intrusion is _____, which includes

such behaviors as snooping through your belongings.

D. Despite common beliefs, dating violence knows no demographic boundaries: men and

women of all _____, _____, _____, and

_____ experience violence in romantic relationships.

    1. If you find yourself in a relationship with a violent partner, let go of the belief that you

can _____ or

_____.

    2. Your only option is to _____.

    3. A(n) _____ is a road map of action for departing the relationship

that provides you with the utmost protection.

E. Five signs of a potentially abusive partner are that he or she will

   1. _____ you from others.

   2. Use _____ to control you.

   3. _____ you in various ways.

   4. Use _____ language.

   5. Shift _____.

WORD SEARCH

Each of the following clues is a key term from Chapter 9. Write the term in the space provided, and then find it hidden in the word search.

1. Suki and Kevin have a wedding ceremony. This is the _____ stage of a relationship.

2. Keith starts working later and later hours so that he won't have to go home and be with his wife. This is an example of the _____ stage of a relationship.

3. Jason and Peter believe that all aspects of their relationship should be fair and balanced. This is an example of _____.

4. Roshanna knows that what she feels for Melvin is deeper than liking him. She feels an intense emotional commitment of intimacy, caring, and attachment known as _____.

5. Sydney sees her boyfriend Wyatt holding hands with another girl. Since this goes against her expectations, it is considered a romantic _____.

6. Ian feels more and more attracted to Tai as they work together. This growing attraction might be caused by the _____ effect.

7. Cerina thinks that she and Vincent were made for each other; they can hardly keep their hands off one another and feel lonely when they're apart even for a few hours. This is an example of _____ love.

8. Karen is distraught to find out that Julie has been spending their retirement money on frivolous things and lying to her about it. The pain and disappointment she feels because Julie doesn't respect her as much as she expected is called _____ devaluation.

```
N W I M Z G J L W Z D E W R R F S X Q J H P
T R T G N Z Q Z G G W H F C E Y S Q H K P H
R J J I F G W J W S N P E S L Q N K E X Z S
T D V V V J O E G A D I Y R A T W Y F T J F
J O R R L R J I S F Q T D S T U R T S X B L
L I K T E E B R A V N D I N I G Q Z K D T M
U V N Y K F V A I A Y E L J O D C O O D U W
Y G O I L O P P T I J E J S N B U O M R C A
G J L F I H J M R H W Z K G A J M J O F W I
H I Q Y E A W Q I E Y A O Q L K H V V Y B A
Y S C G M U Y O A R X X P Q J Z J L Y T Q P
O H U X O S F P U L E M B V K U D X O I J T
J M B O M C Q T M P N L A Y A R T E B U L M
E C V Z T E N A M V A Q I U V A D S N Q W Z
G X C R J D V U L U C S I T F U N T S E E F
N F I Y X O P U B K T Y S A H W D U I I N P
D I N C I L D H O B M Q I I N G D P Q H H P
M N I D O S M U O W U U A E O D I W K K V T
E C I V O K X K E V R C P H K N U A Q V L N
H N Z B Q Y Z G R O K N P N J K A Y B L G F
G A M U E U O O Y M R U P K E O Z T V S W N
M E R E E X P O S U R E U I P S L A E Z N K
```

DEFINING KEY TERMS

Write a sentence that defines each of the following key terms.

1. Companionate love _____

_____

2. Romantic relationship _____

_____

3. Wedging _____

_____

4. Initiating _____

_____

5. Beautiful-is-good effect _____

_____

6. Birds-of-a-feather effect _____

_____

7. Integrating _____

_____

8. Circumscribing _____

_____

9. Relational maintenance _____

_____

10. Relational intrusion _____

_____

11. Romantic betrayal _____

_____

12. Loving _____

_____

CASE STUDY

Read and analyze the following case study, and then answer the questions regarding communication in romantic relationships.

Kristy and Amir have been dating for four years and have fallen into a comfortable but predictable routine. Although their relationship no longer has the "spark" that it once did, Kristy feels a quiet sense of contentment. Amir, however, has been feeling that they are in a rut, that there is no more excitement in their relationship, and that things have become mundane. Because of his negative feelings about their relationship, he has been spending less and less time with Kristy and spending more time with his friends. Then, Kristy gets a new roommate, Sheila. When Amir meets Sheila, he feels that she is pretty in a plain kind of way, and he isn't particularly attracted to her. As Amir sees Sheila more and more when he visits Kristy, he begins to feel drawn to her. Amir begins to e-mail Sheila, and they talk on the phone when Kristy is at work. One day, Kristy happens to see an e-mail from Amir to Sheila stating all of his negative feelings about his relationship with Kristy. Kristy feels betrayed and angry and accuses Amir of being unfaithful. Amir says that Kristy is just jealous and that she has no right to be angry because nothing has happened between him and Sheila.

1. What stages of relational development are Kristy and Amir going through in this scenario?

2. Why do you think Amir begins to feel more and more attracted to Sheila, even though at the beginning he didn't feel that she was exceptionally good-looking?

3. Has Amir cheated on Kristy? Support your answer.

4. Why does Kristy feel so betrayed by Amir? How does emotional devaluation play a role in her feelings?

5. What types of strategies could Kristy and Amir use to approach this problem collaboratively?

SELF-TEST

For each of the following sentences, circle T if the statement is true or F if the statement is false.

T   F   1. Betrayal can be unintentional.

T   F   2. The beautiful-is-good effect states that the more attractive we perceive our romantic partner to be, the harder we try to resolve relationship problems.

T   F   3. Vinny arrives home to find that Margaret has moved out, taking all of her belongings. This is the terminating stage of their relationship.

T   F   4. Addy encourages her new boyfriend to tell her about his fears, and she offers him empathy in return. She is engaged in self-disclosure.

T   F   5. Small talk involves light conversation about "safe" topics.

T   F   6. Relational maintenance is necessary for a relationship to endure.

T   F   7. You can become attracted to someone merely by being around him or her a lot.

T   F   8. In order to encourage relationship talks, one effective strategy is to set aside time in your schedules to chat about your relationship.

T   F   9. Passionate love almost always evolves into companionate love over time.

T   F   10. The most difficult maintenance challenge long-distance couples face is not the separation, but their eventual reunion.

T   F   11. Jealousy is a reaction to a romantic partner's inappropriate behavior.

T   F   12. If you have low self-esteem and feel that you are not very good-looking, according to the matching phenomenon you will have the tendency to be attracted to a person whom you perceive to be not very good-looking as well.

T   F   13. Phillip adores Jean and thinks she is his soul mate. Jean, however, has no clue he feels this way and considers Phillip a friend. Theirs can still be considered a romantic relationship.

T   F   14. According to the text, people seek out romantic partners who make up for the traits they lack.

T   F   15. Social exchange theory states that we are attracted to those who we feel have a lot to offer us with relatively few costs.

T   F   16. The types of romantic love can be described as the varying intensities people can feel in attraction, from liking to obsession.

T   F   17. Being positive in your communication with your romantic partner is an effective relational maintenance tactic.

T   F   18. Whether or not your friends approve of your romantic partner has no effect on your relationship.

T   F   19. Men and women are fundamentally different in the way they perceive and deal with romantic relationships.

T   F   20. Relational intrusion takes place within intact romances only.

Have you ever experienced a romantic betrayal? If yes, how did you choose to deal with that betrayal? If not, suppose you had been romantically betrayed. What strategies would you use to deal with the romantic betrayal?

_____

_____

_____

_____

_____

_____

_____

_____

_____

_____

_____

_____

_____

_____

_____

_____

_____

_____

_____

_____

Name: _____

Class: _____

Date: _____

STUDY OUTLINE

Fill in the blanks to complete the outline.

I. Defining Family

    A. **Family** is a network of people who _____, and

        are bound by marriage, blood, or commitment; who _____as

        family; and who share a significant _____ of

        functioning in a family relationship.

    B. Families possess six common characteristics:

        1. First, families possess a strong sense of _____, created by _____

            _____.

        2. Second, families use communication to define _____, both inside the

            family and to _____ from outsiders.

        3. Third, the _____ underlying family relationships are _____

            _____.

            a. Family members typically hold both _____ and

               _____ feelings toward one another.

4. Fourth, families share a _____.

5. Fifth, family members may share _____.

6. Finally, family members constantly juggle _____ and sometimes _____ roles.

C. Types of Family

1. Sixty years ago, the _____ (a wife, husband, and their biological or adopted children) was the most common family type in North America. Today, it is the _____.

2. When relatives such as aunts, uncles, parents, children, and grandparents live together in a common household, the result is a(n) _____.

3. In a(n) _____, at least one of the adults has a child or children from a previous relationship.

4. _____ consist of two unmarried, romantically involved adults living together in a household, with or without children.

5. In a(n) _____, only one adult resides in the household, possessing sole responsibility as caregiver for the children.

D. Family stories are _____ shared repeatedly within a family that retell historical events and are meant to

_____.

1. _____ stories emphasize the solidity of the parents' relationship, which children find reassuring.

2. _____ stories describe the latter stages of pregnancy, childbirth, and early infancy of a child; these stories can help children understand

_____.

a. Adoptive families share _____ to provide children with a sense of identity and self-esteem.

3. _____ stories relate the coping strategies family members have used to deal with major challenges.

4. To ensure that family stories strengthen, rather than erode, family relationships, select experiences that _____ and that emphasize _____ rather than_____.

II. Communicating in Families

A. According to _____, two dimensions underlie the communication between family members.

1. **Conversation orientation** is the degree to which family members are _____ _____ about a wide array of topics.

2. _____ is the degree to which families believe that communication should emphasize similarity or diversity in attitudes, beliefs, and values.

B. There are four possible family communication patterns:

1. Families high in both conversation and conformity are _____ families.

2. Families high in _____ but low in _____ are **pluralistic families**.

3. **Protective families** are low on conversation and high on _____.

4. Families low in both conversation and conformity are _____families.

III. Maintaining Family Relationships

   A. We often treat family members _____ than we treat individuals

     who have no biological or legal connection to us, but all family relationships need

     _____ to be sustained. Some maintenance strategies include:

     1. Positivity means communicating with your family members in a(n)

       _____ fashion.

     2. Offer regular _____ of how much your family means to you.

     3. _____ in family relationships means sharing your private thoughts

       and feelings with family members and allowing them to do the same without

       _____.

   B. Technology and Family Maintenance

     1. Families typically use online and face-to-face communication in a

       _____, rather than substitutive, fashion.

     2. The biggest advantage of online communication is that it lets you get in touch with

       family members _____.

   C. The two dialectics especially pronounced in families are _____ and

     _____.

     1. The struggle between autonomy and connection is especially difficult to manage during

       _____.

     2. In any close relationship, family bonds included, we want both to share

       _____ and to protect ourselves from

       _____ of such sharing.

a. According to _____, individuals

create informational boundaries by choosing carefully the kind of

_____ they reveal and the people with whom they share it.

b. Family privacy rules are the conditions governing _____

_____, _____ they can discuss such topics, and

who should have access to _____.

IV. Family Relationship Challenges

A. Transitioning to a(n) _____ is a common challenge.

1. The term _____ refers to loyalty conflicts that arise when a

coalition is formed, _____.

2. To help ease the transition to a stepfamily

a. Go slow, but start _____.

b. Practice daily _____.

c. Create new _____.

d. Avoid _____ family members.

e. Be _____.

B. Some parents engage in _____ where one or both parents allocate an

unfair amount of valuable resources to one child over others.

C. **Interparental conflict** involves overt, hostile _____ between

parents in a household.

1. According to the _____, emotions, affect, and mood from

the parental relationship _____ into the broader family, disrupting

children's sense of emotional security.

WORD SEARCH

Each of the following clues is a key term from Chapter 10. Write the term in the space provided, and then find it hidden in the word search.

1. Andre and Kelly are romantic partners and live together, but they are not married. They are an example of a(n) _____ couple.

2. The Price family are trying to decide where to go for their annual family vacation. They believe that they should all agree on the destination. With their high level of conformity and conversation orientation, the Price family are considered a(n) _____ family.

3. Shelly lives in a home with her mother, father, brother, and grandmother. Their household is considered a(n) _____ family.

4. When Corey married Travis, they moved into a home along with Corey's children from his first marriage. Theirs is a(n) _____ family.

5. Kitty's parents never include her in big decisions, and their family never has family talks. Her parents expect her not to deviate too much from the standards they've set for her, and she doesn't have much desire to express herself in family matters. Kitty's family is an example of a(n) _____ family.

6. Ariella attended each one of her son Milo's football games, taking pictures of each play. She went to see her younger son, Micah, play basketball only once during the season. This is known as parental _____.

7. Martin and Shelley are often fighting. Their bad moods and emotions often negatively affect the household at large. This is an example of the _____ hypothesis.

8. Rhea often tells the story of how her two oldest sons used to sit on their younger brother and tickle him until he told them where he hid his candy. This is an example of a family _____.

```
N M R E W Z W J Q U S U Z T E Q T Q K G Q F
B E M X H L H J Y R J P Z V Y Q V T H Q L W
Y Y F T U M Q K O H F C I Q U Y Q B P J A T
U T G E O G R P G G Z T I L K V A W D Y U A
C B S N I O U L W A C L Q Z L Y U G L T S C
G M Q D T R K E R E O B P M G O S X K E N A
H N J E C E J Y T I S A E L J T V J N K E N
F K I D T S Y O K F H R F E O H H E S V S N
L Z F T B A R B V T J Q G R H S A A R E N O
M B D P I P R W Y V L K Y A V X Y W I R O H
F B F K V B X Z T I A Z P H S K B T Z A C O
T S T O H C A C K I B Z U L E M Y F R R J F
Y K Z E V T E H I S L E B L T A U U G F F V
K C O Y W J F Y O H N U C I D D B Z T Q M A
Q B G W F J O L E C U U O P G D K O C U I P
V D U X J N Q H L Z U V C E S O U B R F I C
X S K I D M D J I B C T U F P E T S G L H C
O U T R L M U K V Y A G C X A W S F C Z Q X
W F J P K Z A Y M R T Q X C K H Q G G W L F
K J J L Z K G Z V M K O K H R C Y E R I V D
J F A V O R I T I S M Y F S U L W N A Z O Q
O V A P T L B I N L A N P N I H L O O Y C E
```

DEFINING KEY TERMS

Write a sentence that defines each of the following key terms.

1. Nuclear family _____

   _____

2. Stepfamily _____

   _____

3. Family Communication Patterns Theory _____

   _____

4. Conversation orientation _____

   _____

5. Conformity orientation _____

   _____

6. Pluralistic families _____

   _____

126

7. Laissez-faire families _____

_____

8. Family privacy rules _____

_____

9. Triangulation _____

_____

10. Parental favoritism _____

_____

11. Spillover hypothesis _____

_____

12. Consensual family _____

_____

CASE STUDY

Read and analyze the following case study, and then answer the questions regarding communication in family relationships.

Victoria grew up in a family where children were meant to be seen and not heard. Her parents rarely involved her and her brother in important decisions, and they never had family talks. Her parents discouraged the voicing of opinions because they enforced the idea that the family should all live by traditional values. Because of the absence of communication between Victoria and her parents, they were never aware of her struggle with her identity and just assumed that Victoria's best friend, Deb, was solely that—a friend. But when she was a senior in high school, Victoria shared with her family that she was gay. Victoria also told her parents that her plan was to move out of their house after graduation and move in with Deb and Deb's 1-year-old daughter.

1. Growing up, what was Victoria's family's conversation orientation? What do you think was Victoria's major concern with telling her parents about her sexual orientation?

2. What factors might have made it difficult for Victoria's family to realize that she was gay?

3. Compare and contrast the type of family environment in which Victoria grew up with the type of family she likely will have when she moves in with Deb and her daughter.

4. Given their family communication style, how do you think Victoria's family will react to this news?

5. What communication strategies can Victoria's family use to maintain family relationships?

SELF-TEST

For each of the following sentences, circle T if the statement is true or F if the statement is false.

T   F   1. The majority of families in the United States consist of a mother, a father, and their biological child (or children).

T   F   2. Any couple is considered a type of family.

T   F   3. Family identity is created by how we communicate.

T   F   4. Laissez-faire families are characterized by low levels of conformity and conversation orientation.

T   F   5. The two components of family communication patterns are how much or how little conversation and conformity are expected in the family.

T   F   6. Val, Donn, and Willie often retell the story about how they accidentally set fire to their dad's favorite green chair. This is an example of a family story.

T   F   7. Hallie and Leo live together with their biological daughter, Fia. They are a cohabiting couple.

T   F   8. An extended family is another term for a stepfamily.

T   F   9. Conformity orientation deals with the degree to which family members believe that emotion-sharing is important.

T   F   10. The Rios household consists of a mother, a father, two sons, and a grandmother. This is an example of an extended family.

T   F   11. There are four different family communication patterns: consensual, pluralistic, protective, and laissez-faire.

T   F   12. Consensual families perceive conflict as threatening and seek to address conflicts as they occur.

T   F   13. Family Communication Patterns Theory states that families typically follow the same patterns of conflict and conflict resolutions.

T   F   14. Protective families aim to maintain and enforce existing family norms.

T   F   15. Family privacy rules govern what families talk about, how they talk, and who they can talk to about family information.

T   F   16. Sharing your private thoughts with family members is an important maintenance strategy.

T   F   17. Annie and Howard never discuss finances, their careers, or big decisions with their children. They are a family low in conversation orientation.

T   F   18. Simply communicating in an upbeat and hopeful fashion is a powerful maintenance tactic for families.

T   F   19. Marissa talks to her brother Mark about their childhood dog, Oreo, all the time, but she never talks to her sister Maryann about Oreo because Maryann tends to get very emotional about the topic. This is an example of a family communication pattern.

T   F   20. The tension between autonomy and connection in families refers only to the relationship of children with parents.

JOURNAL ENTRY

Watch an episode of a TV show that involves a family, such as Blue Bloods, Modern Family, *or* The Simpsons. *What is the structure of the onscreen family? What is their typical family communication pattern? What examples do they exhibit of their conversation and conformity orientation? What family communication rules do they exhibit? How is the family's communication part of the show's storytelling?*

_____

_____

_____

_____

_____

_____

_____

_____

_____

_____

_____

_____

_____

_____

_____

_____

_____

_____

Name: _____

Class: _____

Date: _____

STUDY OUTLINE

Fill in the blanks to complete the outline.

I. The Nature of Friendship

    A. **Friendship** is a(n) _____

       characterized by intimacy and liking, and friendship has several distinguishing

       characteristics:

       1. Friendship is _____.

       2. Friendship is driven by _____.

       3. Friendship is characterized by _____.

       4. Friendship is rooted in _____.

       5. Friendship is _____.

    B. Friendships serve many different functions in our lives. Two of the most important are that

       they all help us fulfill our need for _____ and they help

       us _____.

       1. **Communal friendships** focus primarily on sharing _____

          _____ together.

2. In **agentic friendships**, the parties focus primarily on helping each other achieve

_____.

C. The importance we attribute to our friendships _____ throughout our lives.

D. People from different cultures have varied _____ regarding friendships.

E. Friendship beliefs and practices across cultures are also entangled with

_____ norms.

F. Modern technology has changed how friendships are formed and maintained.

1. Communication technologies (e.g., Facebook, etc.) allow people to interact with others

and garner social and emotional support, without suffering _____

_____.

2. Communication technologies make it possible for friends to stay constantly

_____ with each other.

3. Despite currently available technology, people continue to recognize the superiority of

_____and communication.

II. Types of Friendship

A. *Close friends* are people with whom you exchange _____

and _____, share many _____ and

_____, and around whom you feel _____ and

_____.

B. *Best friends* are distinguished by the following characteristics:

1. Best friends typically are _____-sex rather than _____-sex.

2. Best friendship involves greater _____, more

_____, and deeper _____ than close

friendship.

3. People count on their best friends to _____ without judging.

4. The most important factor that distinguishes best friends is unqualified provision of _____, which is defined as behaving in ways that convey _____, _____, and _____ for a friend's **valued social identities**.

    a. Valued social identities are the aspects of your public self that you deem the most important in _____.

C. People regularly forge friendships that cross demographic lines, known as **cross-category friendships**. Four types of cross-category friendships are:

1. Cross-_____ friendships.

2. Cross-_____ friendships.

3. _____ friendships.

4. _____ friendships.

III. Maintaining Friendships

A. We can help our friendships succeed by following friendship rules—general principles that prescribe appropriate _____ and _____ within friendship relationships. There are 10 rules:

1. Show _____.

2. Seek _____.

3. Respect _____.

4. Keep _____.

5. _____ your friends.

6. Avoid public _____.

7. Make your friends _____.

8. Manage _____.

9. Share _____.

10. Maintain _____.

B. Most friendships are built on a foundation of _____ and

_____.

1. Through _____, friends structure their schedules to enjoy

hobbies, interests, and leisure activities together.

2. All friendships are created and maintained through the discussion of

_____, _____, and

_____.

IV. Friendship Challenges

A. Acts of friendship betrayal include _____,

_____ (criticizing a friend behind his or her back),

_____, and _____.

B. _____ is one of the most common and intense challenges friends face.

1. In friendships that survive geographic distance, the two people feel a particularly strong

_____.

2. To communicate in ways that foster positive qualities in a long-distance friendship, use

_____.

C. A final challenge facing friends is _____ to one another beyond

friendship: _____, _____, or both.

1. Friends who feel attracted to one another typically report high

_____ as a result, both regarding the nature of their

relationship and whether or not their friend _____.

2. Ways to cope with the attraction include:

a. Simply _____ the attraction, perhaps by engaging in

_____.

b. Act on the attraction by either developing a(n)

_____ or trying to blend friendship

with sexual activity through a _____

arrangement.

3. When transitioning from a friendship to romance, expect

_____, emphasize _____, and offer

_____.

4. In **FWB relationships** ("friends-with-benefits" relationships), participants

_____, but not with the purpose of

transforming the relationship into a(n) _____.

a. Both men *and* women form FWB relationships for two reasons: they welcome the

lack of _____ and they want to satisfy _____

_____.

b. The majority of FWB relationships eventually _____.

WORD SEARCH

Each of the following clues is a key term from Chapter 11. Write the term in the space provided, and then find it hidden in the word search.

1. Gossiping about a friend behind his or her back or lying to him or her is considered friendship

   _____.

2. Happy provides her best friend, Rowan, unqualified _____ support as a fitness

   instructor, conveying her understanding and acceptance.

3. Anson believes that through his _____ friendship with Elisa

   he can gain a better understanding of how the other sex thinks, feels, and behaves.

4. Defending your friends is an important friendship _____.

5. Roger and Liza have agreed that they will remain strictly friends, but once in a while they

   engage in sexual activity. This is an example of a(n) _____ relationship.

6. Regina and Rose are friends who go out to lunch together once a week, play tennis

   on the weekends, and talk on the telephone every night. This is an example of a(n)

   _____ friendship.

7. When Lee and Bren formed a study group for school, they formed a(n) _____

   friendship.

8. Michael, who is a Euro-American from Michigan, never met anyone from India until

   he was assigned Ravi, who was born in New Delhi, as a college roommate. Discovering

   a shared interest in techno music, they are now very close. Theirs is an example of a(n)

   _____ friendship.

```
R I B D G M O O V B J I J F Z G I K L A I X
J W W Z Q R Q V Y K E Q R C E W H G T I D S
F B M Y U I H Z M Y T T T V D Q F T W G E D
Q N S N I Z U C C O T K R C J G H K V W N U
Y C Q E D S R M W U B T C A D G X W F X T K
C L R A Y O K P M Y X L N N Y D G Y T D I H
X G Y F S L T F N Q I K G K C A C M E Y T J
K I S S Q K G J Q U J T S Z M H L K D Q Y E
B S S T O X L Y F L N V J U E E V M F T C Q
C E Q G Y A L N M M Y N H Z B N K V B Y E P
X T J U H F M A G V L D B D M C I S M Q F C
P A M Q I W Y K Z K W B R N N Q I V U T Y F
Z E Q C N L O M H Q X X S D E I H T N Z B V
C R O S S C U L T U R A L B E J K N N X D F
Y F Q S L V T U P V X D C U L V F W U E Y U
L F N M I F W S A B R R D Y U V D L C F G N
U Y E H S R T S P Z J P Y B R Y O B Y A J A
S Y F N L M V G Q Z A O I K U R W I O S A F
V L M B C Q E S F E F Q P A B I D V R P B E
I R D C D V F N J B T E S F L A N U M M O C
Y X V D V Y E D T L D B B Q G W E S Y H Q J
F D P J T B P N H Q J S F Q H J H N O B V E
```

DEFINING KEY TERMS

Write a sentence that defines each of the following key terms.

1. Friendship _____

   _____

2. Communal friendships _____

   _____

3. Agentic friendships _____

   _____

4. Identity support _____

   _____

5. Valued social identities _____

   _____

6. Cross-category friendships _____

   _____

7. Friendship rules _____

_____

8. FWB relationships _____

CASE STUDY

Read and analyze the following case study, and then answer the questions regarding communication in relationships with friends.

Drew and Jace met in fifth grade. They grew up living down the street from one another and played baseball together. They were the best of friends throughout high school, sharing their dreams, fears, and deepest secrets. They went to separate colleges, though they still kept in touch through Facebook and e-mail and publicly referred to each other as "best friend." During their third year in college, Drew told Jace he would be dropping out of college to pursue his lifelong dream of becoming a professional baseball player. Jace did not support Drew's decision and tried to convince Drew that playing baseball is a thing of the past and that Drew should give up the notion of ever becoming a professional baseball player. Drew was devastated and began to question his friendship with Jace.

1. How was Drew and Jace's friendship typical for adolescence?

2. Would you classify Jace as Drew's best friend in childhood? Why or why not? Did this change during the course of their lifespan? How?

3. What could Drew and Jace have done to better maintain their friendship across the geographic distance?

4. How does the concept of valued social identities play a role in Drew and Jace's situation?

5. Do you think situations like the one above are common? Why or why not?

SELF-TEST

For each of the following sentences, circle T if the statement is true or F if the statement is false.

T   F   1. Friendship is characterized by intimacy and liking.

T   F   2. Natalie and Bertie's interests have diverged a great deal in the past few years and they now have very little in common. This is a typical reason why friendships end.

T   F   3. Friendships can happen involuntarily.

T   F   4. Romantic relationships are more likely to change and break off than friendships.

T   F   5. Sue helps Michelle do her taxes. In turn, Michelle walks Sue's dog. Their friendship is limited to these activities. Theirs is an agentic friendship.

T   F   6. Communal friendships involve two people who share living space or resources.

T   F   7. Shea and Jade enjoy going shopping, drinking coffee, and going on long walks with each other. This is an example of an agentic friendship.

T   F   8. The importance of friendship wanes drastically for married men.

T   F   9. Men and women value the importance of both kinds of friendships equally.

T   F   10. Through technology, you can form friendships quickly and with more people.

T   F   11. Seba's 1,396 Facebook "friends" are probably all true friends.

T   F   12. Padma avoids going to the bar with Aaron because she is attracted to him and she doesn't want to engage in activities that might inadvertently lead to sexual interaction. She is using a mental management strategy.

T   F   13. Friends-with-benefits relationships normally work out well if there are clear rules about the friendship from the beginning.

T   F   14. Typically, communication technologies may help maintain friendships that face geographic separation.

T   F   15. One of the differences between family relationships and friendships is that friendships are voluntary.

T   F   16. Sean and Norman work out together on a regular basis, helping "spot" each other while lifting weights, motivating each other, and giving each other fitness tips. They never spend time together outside the gym. This is an agentic relationship.

T   F   17. A promise to not pursue the attraction one has for a friend is a form of mental management.

T   F   18. Seeking revenge against a friend who has betrayed you can serve as an effective betrayal management strategy.

T   F   19. Both men and women report that being able to freely and deeply disclose is *the* defining feature of friendship.

T   F   20. By the sixth grade, same-sex friends have become our primary source of emotional support over our families.

JOURNAL ENTRY

Think about your longest-standing friendship. How was the friendship forged? Have you encountered any friendship challenges, such as betrayal, separation, or attraction? What strategies have you used to maintain the friendship?

_____

_____

_____

_____

_____

_____

_____

_____

_____

_____

_____

_____

_____

_____

_____

_____

_____

<table>
<tr><td rowspan="3">

CHAPTER 12

Relationships in the Workplace

</td><td>Name: _____</td></tr>
<tr><td>Class: _____</td></tr>
<tr><td>Date: _____</td></tr>
</table>

STUDY OUTLINE

Fill in the blanks to complete the outline.

I. Defining Workplace Relationships

   A. A **workplace relationship** is any _____

   _____.

      1. These involvements differ along three dimensions: _____,

      _____, and _____.

   B. **Organizational culture** derives from three sources:

      1. *Workplace values* are _____

      _____.

      2. *Workplace norms* are guidelines governing _____

      _____.

      3. *Workplace artifacts*, which also contribute to an organization's culture, are

      _____.

   C. _____, or systems of communication linkages, are defined

   by three characteristics:

1. The first characteristic is the _____ that flows

   through the network.

2. The second characteristic is the _____ through which the

   information flows.

3. The third is the frequency and number of connections among people in a network, also

   known as _____.

4. _____ are groups of coworkers linked solely through e-mail,

   social networking sites, Skype, and other Internet destinations.

5. _____ are dense networks of coworkers who share the same

   workplace values and broader life attitudes.

II. Organizational Climates

   A. A workplace's **organizational climate** is created primarily through

   _____, specifically, the amount of _____,

   _____, _____, and _____ present in the

   interactions between organizational members.

   B. In a **defensive climate**, the environment is _____

   _____.

   C. In a **supportive climate**, the workplace is _____, _____,

   and _____.

   D. Some strategies for creating a supportive climate are:

   1. Encourage _____.

   2. Adopt _____.

   3. _____ rather than _____.

4. Describe _____ rather than _____.

5. Offer _____ rather than _____.

6. Emphasize _____.

III. Technology in the Workplace

A. _____ in the workplace provides substantial

advantages over face-to-face and phone interactions.

B. The biggest advantage of communication technologies within the workplace is that

_____ , in a relational fashion.

C. Workers in the United States now spend almost two hours a day **cyberslacking**, which is

defined as using their work computers to _____

_____, when they should be focused on work tasks.

IV. Peer Relationships

A. **Professional peers** are _____

_____.

1. *Information peers* are _____

_____

_____.

2. *Collegial peers* are _____.

3. *Special peers* are _____

_____

_____.

4. **Virtual peers** are _____

_____.

B. _____ and _____ are important tactics in maintaining peer relationships.

   1. Giving _____ to collegial and special peers helps demonstrate your commitment to them.

   2. Collegial and special peer relationships also grow stronger when the people involved treat one another as _____ and do not strictly define each other as just _____.

V. Mixed-Status Relationships

A. **Mixed-status relationships** are defined as relationships between _____ _____.

   1. For example, in *supervisory relationships*, one person _____ and _____ another.

B. **Upward communication** is communication from _____.

C. The most effective form of upward communication is _____, which is based on six principles:

   1. Plan before you _____.

   2. Know why your supervisor should _____.

   3. Tailor your _____.

   4. Know your supervisor's _____.

   5. Create coalitions _____.

   6. Competently _____.

D. **Downward communication** comprises messages that people with formal authority use when _____.

E. Effective downward communication involves five principles:

   1. Routinely and openly emphasize the _____ in workplace

      relationships with subordinates.

   2. _____ empathetically.

   3. Frame wants and needs as _____.

   4. Be sensitive to your _____.

   5. Share _____ with employees whenever possible.

F. How to effectively _____ subordinates and how to

   _____ them are two challenges of downward communication.

   1. Compliments are most effective when they focus on a subordinate's _____;

      avoid compliments about _____.

   2. To offer constructive criticism:

      a. Open your interaction with _____ and end with

         _____.

      b. Follow the guidelines for _____ and

         _____.

G. Maintaining mixed-status relationships requires you to _____

   _____

   _____ and to communicate in _____

   _____ ways.

VI. Challenges to Workplace Relationships

A. **Workplace bullying** is the repeated _____

   _____.

1. When bullying occurs online, it is known as _____.

2. Bullying typically generates feelings of _____, _____, and _____. It can even cause health problems such as _____, _____, and _____.

3. Workplace bullying has six common forms:

    a. _____ (e.g., restriction of interaction).

    b. Control of _____.

    c. Constraint of _____.

    d. Creation of _____.

    e. _____ abuse.

    f. Destruction of _____.

B. A second challenge to workplace relationships is the development of _____ for coworkers.

    1. Many of the elements that foster attraction are present in the workplace, such as a wide variety of _____, large amounts of _____, physical _____, and similarity of _____.

    2. The negative outcomes associated with workplace romances are more pronounced for _____ than for _____.

    3. You can successfully overcome the challenge of maintaining a workplace romance by communicating with your partner in a(n) _____ _____ during work hours, and by using

e-mail, text, Facebook, and instant messaging judiciously to _____ your

relationship.

C. **Sexual harassment** occurs in two forms in the workplace.

1. In *quid pro quo harassment*, a person in a supervisory position asks for or demands

_____ in return for _____

_____.

2. *Hostile climate harassment* is _____ intended to disrupt a

person's _____.

3. Some ways of coping with sexual harassment are _____ the harasser,

_____ the harasser, or interpreting the harassment in ways that

_____.

4. Confronting harassers is strongly encouraged as a matter of principle, but the

_____ can be hard to manage.

5. If you're not sure what to do, contact the _____.

WORD SEARCH

Each of the following clues is a key term from Chapter 12. Write the term in the space provided, and then find it hidden in the word search.

1. Russell tries to persuade his office manager, Peter, to implement a new training schedule for the

new employees. This is an example of _____.

2. Leon and Monica are coworkers who communicate via instant messaging all day. They are

_____ peers.

3. Amanda, Glen, Mario, and Osmond are considered the young, hip, carefree group at their

workplace. Their group is an example of a workplace _____.

4. Karen asks her boss for two weeks off. This is an example of _____ communication.

5. Jin and Tran both hold the title of Education Specialist II at their workplace. They are considered professional _____.

6. Aries, the restaurant manager, asks Jamie, a food server, to pick up his dry cleaning. When Jamie reluctantly agrees, Aries thanks her and slaps her on the behind. This is an example of _____ harassment.

7. Karina takes credit for the annual charity dinner that Emery planned and organized. This is an example of a workplace _____.

8. At VBS Business Solutions, employees feel discouraged and unsupported, and employee morale is low. This is a(n) _____ climate.

```
E F A E W J V I R T U A L D K M P Q R S J C
V C K M K R H D U Q G W S U F F I P P A P J
I N O H X G Q I C Z Q E U M T W V L Y I M S
S X K R E O R R W H X D R H I M K U A Z L M
N R A M E L N W Q U M F K E N J O J L M P Z
E J S K L R Z C A D R W D J E F U F J Q Q W
F H N G D Z Z L P H J O Z Y D L Z I A V A Z
E D O O G V C K P M O H P U B S P F Z N R R
D N U N P O N T T X H I K X S D K Z Y J Q N
B J I P P B M V O U Q U N L L H O C G P I E
S R E E P D Q I F K Y E P T V A A T K Y Z D
N X H Y C E N F T H H X Y C Z C Q M O X J D
C E M P G T T U J G I V D G O L D O F B D J
W L S K K T E P G C N S F V K X Q R T Z K O
P G I U J P B W M A T M D U X B F X N H B V
V N H Q B P L A H N K A O L Q X C A Q V S N
L S L J U A E R D M L H X G I R L G N W U Q
E P S W V E B D I C D F T P S L N D O S O S
B X A K D L N U N Z W D P Q P H D D D R K Q
A E R I B W S Q F J R W L C H Q N D P R R D
Q T F I T P Q R F B S D C X Y L H G J Y U W
I T K H X C K G E A U S Y G O R X G C L O V
```

DEFINING KEY TERMS

Write a sentence that defines each of the following key terms.

1. Workplace relationships _____

   _____

2. Organizational culture _____

   _____

3. Organizational networks _____

   _____

4. Virtual networks _____

   _____

5. Organizational climate _____

   _____

6. Supportive climate _____

   _____

7. Mixed-status relationships _____

   _____

8. Downward communication _____

   _____

9. Advocacy _____

   _____

10. Workplace bullying _____

    _____

11. Sexual harassment _____

    _____

12. Virtual peers _____

    _____

CASE STUDY

Read and analyze the following case study, and then answer the questions regarding communication in workplace relationships.

Trey is a lead engineer at a biotechnology firm. He supervises a group of four engineers and reports to Irene, the director of engineering. Trey and Irene have gotten along very well since Trey started working for the firm. Trey is an ambitious go-getter with a professional, positive attitude, as is Irene. Trey, Irene, and a few other upper- and middle-management employees often hang out outside of work. Due to recent budget concerns, the firm has begun to lay off some employees. Irene has empathetically and politely requested that Trey lay off two of the engineers who work under him. Trey does as he is asked. Weeks later, Trey's two remaining subordinates begin to complain to Trey about the workload. They claim that they have absorbed the work of the two laid-off employees and blame the upper management, including Irene. They have been heard talking maliciously about the upper management in the break room and in the parking lot. Trey is conflicted because even though he doesn't agree with the manner in which his subordinates are handling the matter, he knows that they are, indeed, under a great amount of stress given the increased workload. Trey is unsure about what, if anything, to tell Irene.

1. What type of peer relationship exists between Trey and Irene? How does this affect their communication about work matters?

2. Describe how the formation and existence of workplace cliques play a role in this scenario.

3. What strategies can Trey utilize in this scenario to effectively maintain his relationship with Irene?

4. How might the behavior of Trey's two remaining subordinates affect the workplace culture?

5. How could Trey's two remaining subordinates communicate their concerns in a more constructive way?

SELF-TEST

For each of the following sentences, circle T if the statement is true or F if the statement is false.

T F 1. Workplace cliques always contribute to a decrease in worker productivity.

T F 2. Workplace cliques are defined as coworkers who interact regularly together outside the workplace.

T F 3. Organizational climates can be either defensive or supportive but not both.

T F 4. Downward communication is defined as talking down to employees or being condescending.

T F 5. Sherwin and Ephraim are a couple who work at the same company. This is an example of a mixed-status relationship.

T F 6. Advocacy means standing up for what you think is right.

T F 7. Advanced Biometrics is a company that values working hard and playing hard. This mentality is part of the organizational culture.

T F 8. Doug, Lou, Lynn, and Mari are all on the "counselor list" on the company e-mail system, and they communicate regularly but only through e-mail. Theirs is a virtual network.

T   F   9. Workplace relationships differ along three dimensions: status, intimacy, and equity.

T   F   10. Quyen feels that she deserves a raise but is afraid to ask her boss because she feels he is unfriendly and inflexible, just like the company as a whole. This is an example of a defensive climate.

T   F   11. Suzie and Miguel have daily debriefings to update each other on the status of their projects. This is an organizational network.

T   F   12. Balance Credit Systems has an annual family picnic and gives all employees the day off, paid. This is a way for the company to help build a supportive climate.

T   F   13. Upward communication travels from subordinate to superior.

T   F   14. Cynthia repeatedly sends Carrie e-mails belittling her work at the office. This is an example of workplace bullying.

T   F   15. Workplace bullying often stems from the power difference in mixed-status relationships.

T   F   16. Workplace artifacts are physical objects that contribute to an organization's culture.

T   F   17. The negative outcomes associated with workplace romances may be more pronounced for men than for women.

T   F   18. Effective downward communication is characterized by the willingness of people in power to communicate positively without relying on their power.

T   F   19. Supervisors should not phrase wants and needs as requests because doing so relinquishes power.

T   F   20. Floyd's boss often demands that he finish reports that normally take two to three hours in twenty minutes. This unreasonable request is a form of workplace bullying.

JOURNAL ENTRY

What do you think are the most important factors in building a positive working environment? Do you think that employee interaction outside the workplace helps or hinders productivity? Support your ideas, and cite specific examples.

ANSWER KEY

CHAPTER 1

1.	T	(p. 7)	8.	T	(p. 10)	15.	F	(p. 16)
2.	F	(p. 11)	9.	T	(p. 11)	16.	T	(p. 13)
3.	F	(p. 13)	10.	F	(p. 13)	17.	F	(p. 26)
4.	F	(p. 8)	11.	T	(p. 13)	18.	T	(p. 28)
5.	F	(p. 9)	12.	T	(pp. 23–24)	19.	F	(p. 15)
6.	T	(p. 8)	13.	F	(p. 14)	20.	F	(p. 23)
7.	F	(p. 9)	14.	T	(p. 18)			

CHAPTER 2

1.	F	(p. 50)	8.	F	(p. 57)	15.	T	(p. 62)
2.	F	(p. 52)	9.	F	(p. 65)	16.	F	(pp. 63–64)
3.	T	(p. 61)	10.	T	(p. 69)	17.	F	(p. 43)
4.	T	(p. 52)	11.	T	(p. 50)	18.	T	(p. 55)
5.	F	(p. 39)	12.	F	(p. 68)	19.	T	(p. 57)
6.	T	(p. 46)	13.	F	(p. 65)	20.	F	(p. 52)
7.	T	(p. 59)	14.	T	(p. 52)			

CHAPTER 3

1.	F	(pp. 95–96)	8.	T	(p. 77)	15.	F	(p. 87)
2.	T	(p. 81)	9.	T	(p. 101)	16.	F	(pp. 88–89)
3.	F	(p. 99)	10.	T	(p. 101)	17.	T	(p. 92)
4.	T	(p. 84)	11.	T	(p. 83)	18.	T	(p. 96)
5.	F	(pp. 77–78)	12.	F	(pp. 90–91)	19.	F	(p. 101)
6.	T	(p. 93)	13.	F	(pp. 93–94)	20.	F	(p. 95)
7.	T	(p. 76)	14.	T	(p. 87)			

CHAPTER 4

1.	F	(p. 113)	8.	F	(p. 125)	15.	T	(p. 126)
2.	T	(p. 128)	9.	T	(pp. 131–132)	16.	F	(p. 126)
3.	T	(p. 119)	10.	F	(p. 125)	17.	T	(p. 134)
4.	F	(p. 131)	11.	T	(pp. 123, 125)	18.	T	(p. 135)
5.	T	(p. 115)	12.	T	(pp. 129–130)	19.	T	(p. 128)
6.	T	(p. 134)	13.	T	(p. 113)	20.	T	(p. 114)
7.	T	(p. 126)	14.	T	(p. 123)			

Chapter 5

1.	T	(p. 160)	8.	T	(p. 153)	15.	T	(p. 161)
2.	T	(p. 167)	9.	F	(p. 148)	16.	F	(p. 167)
3.	F	(pp. 148–149)	10.	F	(p. 150)	17.	T	(p. 152)
4.	T	(p. 153)	11.	T	(p. 152)	18.	T	(p. 161)
5.	F	(p. 157)	12.	F	(p. 151)	19.	F	(p. 149)
6.	F	(p. 161)	13.	T	(p. 156)	20.	T	(p. 148)
7.	F	(p. 166)	14.	T	(p. 170)			

Chapter 6

1.	T	(p. 178)	8.	T	(p. 181)	15.	T	(p. 177)
2.	T	(p. 187)	9.	F	(p. 194)	16.	T	(p. 193)
3.	F	(p. 177)	10.	T	(p. 186)	17.	F	(p. 194)
4.	F	(p. 179)	11.	T	(p. 198)	18.	F	(p. 179)
5.	F	(p. 184)	12.	T	(p. 179)	19.	F	(p. 186)
6.	T	(p. 191)	13.	T	(p. 179)	20.	F	(p. 193)
7.	T	(p. 193)	14.	F	(p. 179)			

Chapter 7

1.	T	(p. 213)	8.	T	(p. 229)	15.	F	(p. 223)
2.	T	(p. 234)	9.	T	(p. 220)	16.	T	(p. 220)
3.	F	(p. 218)	10.	F	(p. 234)	17.	T	(p. 223)
4.	T	(p. 224)	11.	T	(p. 229)	18.	F	(pp. 220, 234)
5.	T	(p. 213)	12.	T	(p. 235)	19.	T	(p. 213)
6.	F	(p. 227)	13.	F	(p. 219)	20.	T	(p. 221)
7.	F	(p. 225)	14.	T	(p. 226)			

Chapter 8

1.	F	(p. 257)	8.	T	(p. 258)	15.	F	(pp. 257–258)
2.	T	(p. 258)	9.	F	(p. 262)	16.	T	(p. 260)
3.	T	(p. 257)	10.	F	(p. 256)	17.	T	(p. 247)
4.	T	(p. 249)	11.	T	(p. 251)	18.	F	(p. 268)
5.	F	(p. 249)	12.	T	(p. 266)	19.	T	(p. 256)
6.	T	(p. 255)	13.	F	(p. 252)	20.	T	(pp. 265–266)
7.	T	(p. 268)	14.	T	(p. 251)			

CHAPTER 9

1.	F	(p. 307)	8.	T	(p. 303)	15.	T	(p. 291)
2.	F	(p. 290)	9.	T	(p. 284)	16.	F	(p. 284)
3.	T	(p. 297)	10.	T	(p. 304)	17.	T	(p. 300)
4.	F	(p. 302)	11.	F	(p. 310)	18.	F	(p. 303)
5.	T	(p. 294)	12.	T	(p. 290)	19.	F	(p. 283)
6.	T	(p. 300)	13.	F	(p. 291)	20.	F	(p. 312)
7.	T	(p. 289)	14.	F	(p. 290)			

CHAPTER 10

1.	F	(pp. 323, 325)	8.	F	(p. 326)	15.	T	(p. 339)
2.	F	(p. 324)	9.	F	(p. 330)	16.	F	(p. 335)
3.	T	(p. 323)	10.	T	(p. 326)	17.	T	(p. 330)
4.	T	(p. 333)	11.	T	(p. 331)	18.	T	(p. 335)
5.	T	(p. 331)	12.	T	(p. 332)	19.	F	(p. 330)
6.	T	(p. 326)	13.	F	(p. 330)	20.	F	(p. 337)
7.	T	(p. 326)	14.	T	(p. 333)			

CHAPTER 11

1.	T	(p. 355)	8.	T	(p. 358)	15.	T	(p. 355)
2.	T	(p. 356)	9.	T	(p. 359)	16.	T	(p. 357)
3.	F	(p. 355)	10.	T	(p. 360)	17.	T	(p. 376)
4.	F	(p. 357)	11.	F	(p. 360)	18.	F	(p. 373)
5.	T	(p. 357)	12.	T	(p. 376)	19.	T	(p. 356)
6.	F	(p. 357)	13.	F	(p. 377)	20.	F	(p. 358)
7.	F	(p. 357)	14.	T	(p. 374)			

CHAPTER 12

1.	F	(p. 391)	8.	T	(p. 390)	15.	T	(p. 402)
2.	F	(p. 391)	9.	F	(p. 387)	16.	T	(p. 389)
3.	F	(p. 393)	10.	T	(p. 392)	17.	F	(p. 410)
4.	F	(p. 402)	11.	T	(p. 390)	18.	T	(p. 403)
5.	F	(p. 400)	12.	T	(p. 392)	19.	F	(p. 403)
6.	F	(p. 400)	13.	T	(p. 400)	20.	T	(p. 408)
7.	T	(p. 389)	14.	T	(p. 407)